Guide to Protecting Your Teen Against Internet Predators

Rodney Alexander

outskirtspress

DENVER, COLORADO

Contents

Abstract

TEENAGE INTERNET USERS are the fastest growing segment in the Internet user population. These
teenagers are at risk of sexual assault from Internet
predators. This guide explores teacher and counselors' perceptions of how to prevent this sexual assault.
Twenty-five teacher and counselor participants were
interviewed. A modified van Kaam method was used
to analyze the data and develop themes. Participants
stated that mainly the lack of parental support and
social networking website were the circumstances
leading to teenage Internet sexual assault, while teen
needs and gratification usually played a role in teen
encounters with predators on the Internet. There were
13 emergent themes in this guide and those themes
were; lack of parental support, anonymity on the
Internet, teenage loneliness, social networking websites and chat rooms, teenage personality (introversive
and extroversive), teenage rebellion, teenage need

for relationships, instant gratification among teenagers, teenage low self-esteem, improved parental support, improved education, improved law enforcement and additional circumstances leading to the teenage Internet sexual assault phenomenon.

Acknowledgements

A GUIDE IS a team project with many players, coaches, and supportive fans.

I am fortunate to have had the skilled and knowledgeable coaching of Dr. Karen Johnson, Dr. Jiefeng Xu, and Dr. Olufemi Akintunde. I extend my thanks and admiration to each of them for skillfully guiding me through this process. I am moved by the generosity of the Midwestern United States town High School teachers and counselors in my guide, amazed by their tenacity, and their dedication to the teenagers through difficult experiences. They are on the field of life and make the tough plays of counseling teenagers safely through many challenges. I offer my thanks and prayers to each of them and the teenagers.

CHAPTER **1**

Overview

THE INTERNET HAS become very important in society; it is present in the majority of households in America, but it is also becoming a new venue for sexual predators. According to van Manen (2010) sharing personal information (online) can be unexpectedly risky—in part because sexual predators and pedophiles prey on unsuspecting social network users. Places such as chat rooms are becoming places where child predators meet 13 to 17 year olds in order to solicit them for sex. According to Wolak, David, Mitchell, and Ybarra (2008), the Internet is becoming an increasingly dangerous place for children.

Social networking websites such as Facebook®, MySpace™, Twitter© and instant messaging can open the door for teen exploitation on the Internet. For example, according to anonymous (2011) the federal authorities are seeking access to multiple e-mail and Facebook® accounts, including some bearing the name of slain North Carolina teen Phylicia Barnes, as part of a child pornography and sexual exploitation of children investigation. This guide may increase the knowledge in the law enforcement, educator, mental health professionals and the parental community on how to reduce this relatively new threat to children.

An exhaustive review of the literature helped to determine that the current available research does not provide adequate information to educators, parents, mental health professionals and law enforcement. It is also inadequate when educating 13 to 17 year-olds on how to avoid predators on the Internet. This guide consists of interviews with teachers/counselors who have worked with teen victims of sexual assault from someone whom they met on the Internet.

Environment

Chat rooms and social networking websites such as Facebook®, MySpace™ and Twitter© are places where Internet predators often go to solicit teens for sex. According to Bower (2008) most of online sex offenders are adults who contact vulnerable 13 to 17 year-olds and seduce them into sexual relationships. Teens are being seduced by predators using the Internet. Adult predators use social websites such as Facebook®, MySpace™ and Twitter© to entice teens into sexual activity.

According to Dylan and Fuller (2010) the Facebook® management repeatedly failed to reveal the activity of an international child pornography syndicate operating on their site. Teens inadvertently post personal information on these sites that predators often use to entice them into a sexual relationship. According to Shao (2009) individuals participate [on the Internet] through interacting with the content as well as with other users for enhancing social connections and virtual communities; and they produce their own contents for self-expression and self-actualization.

Teenagers are often seeking gratification via the Internet and these adults take advantage of those who are seeking relationships on the Internet. Posting personal information on the Internet provides pleasure and satisfaction for many teens. User-generated media (UGM) like YouTube, MySpace, and Wikipedia have become tremendously popular over the last few years (Shao, 2009).

Social websites such as Facebook®, MySpace™ and Twitter© serve as teen social gathering places to share photos and exchange gossip. According to Peter, Valkenburg, Schouten and Alexander (2005) the Internet [is seen] as a new social environment in which universal adolescent issues such as identity, sexuality, and a sense of self-worth are played out in a virtual world. The virtual reality of the Internet presents a location for teens to fulfill their fantasies. An influential tradition in media research, U&G presents media use in terms of the gratification or psychological needs of the individual (Shao, 2009).

Social needs of the individual are often satisfied by social media. This new social environment is growing not only in the United States, but globally, as well. It has become woven into the everyday activity of most teens. Teenage Internet use has become prevalent worldwide. According to Shannon (2008) a recent study of Swedish children's media habits found that 95% of 12 to 16 year-olds use the Internet and that 28% and 54%, respectively, use the Internet every day.

The increased number of teens using the Internet increases the probability that they are likely to meet a predator. Online sexual assault among juveniles seems to be prevalent among teenagers and less so among younger children. Children coming into contact with Internet predators become increasingly common as children approach and enter their teenage years (Shannon, 2008).

The Internet is increasingly becoming the location where predators meet kids as they grow into teenagers. Nissley (2008) reported that the Internet is increasingly becoming the method in which predators meet teen victims, stating that between 2000 and 2001 most predators used the Internet to develop relationships with children to meet them for sex. About five percent of offenders pretended to be teens while developing relationships with teens online, often enter chat rooms to meet them.

This guide may help to develop different approaches

for combating teen sexual assault on the Internet. Strategies that target 13 to 17 year olds directly and acknowledge normal adolescent interests in romance and sex are needed (Wolak et al., 2008). Age driven educational strategies are necessary for teens to help them avoid online predators.

These educational strategies can directly target this new teen Internet sexual assault phenomenon. Successful educational strategies can help prevent this antisocial behavior. Preventing school failure can act to reduce exposure to other environmental influences contributing to antisocial behavior and to reduce expression of both genetic and non-shared environmental influences on antisocial behavior (Johnson et al., 2009). Parents, teachers, mental health professionals, and law enforcement also need additional data to better understand this growing form of assault against teenagers. Teen Internet sexual assault is a growing problem for society, one that requires understanding of the type of gratification that teens gain from using the Internet and how to prevent the seeking of that gratification from leading to sexual assault. Studies have shown that a low grade point average (GPA) is one factor associated with teen antisocial behavior.

Very low age 17 GPA encouraged expression of genetically influenced antisocial behavior and that something about high GPA minimized expression of these genetic and environmental influences on antisocial behavior (Johnson et al., 2009). New approaches are needed to help prevent the increasing sexual assaults against teens on the Internet. Prevention approaches take into consideration the nuances of the Internet such as personal information protection, and the control of personal relationships on the Internet.

Hypothetical Attention

Teenagers use the Internet more than adults. According to van den Eijnden, Spijkerman, Vermulst, van Rooij, and Engels, (2010) adolescents aged 14 and older regard Internet use as a more important leisure time activity than watching television. Not only do teens use the Internet more, they also use Internet tools such as social websites and chat rooms more than adults. Parents are focusing more attention on protecting their teens from the vices that exist on the Internet.

The rising popularity of the internet and the ever increasing amount of time adolescents spend online pose challenges to parents who want to protect their teenage children from excessive internet use (van den Eijnden et al., 2010). The Internet plays an important role in the social lives of teens. These new forms of communications offer greater opportunity for predators to meet and engage teenagers on the Internet. Adolescents may develop an uncontrollable urge to use the Internet, often accompanied by a loss of control, a preoccupation with internet use, and continued use despite negative consequences (van den Eijnden et al., 2010).

Social networking sites such as Facebook®, MySpace™ and Twitter© also offer anonymity for both the teenager and the predator. This anonymity may decrease inhibition for both the teenager and a potential predator. Further research is needed on the role of anonymity and reduced cues in the teen Internet sexual assault phenomenon. Currently, there are two theories that address why teenagers seek relationships on the Internet.

Scholars have put forward two opposing hypotheses on the relationship between introversion/extraversion and online friendship formation (Peter et al., 2005). Both introverted and extroverted teens could fall victim to sexual predators on the Internet. The two opposing hypotheses are the rich-get-richer and the social compensation hypothesis.

According to the rich-get-richer hypothesis, because contact can be made more easily online, extroverted teens use their enhanced social skills to develop friendships in chat rooms and on social networking sites (Peter et al., 2005). This theory states that extroverted teens will have more success at using the Internet than introverted teens. The rich-get-richer hypothesis states that the Internet will primarily benefit extroverted individuals (Peter et al., 2005).

Using the Internet, extroverted teens may practice meeting people, consequently enhancing their ability to make friends. According to the rich-get-richer theory, extroverted teens are more likely than introverts to

establish relationships online. A teen's ability to establish relationships online may lead to teens establishing relationships with Internet predators. Extroverted
teens may feel an increase in self-esteem when they
successfully meet someone online.

Lee (2009) stated that extroverted teens felt better
when they used the Internet; they felt more confident
and felt less isolated. Extroverted teens felt as though
they were part of a social group, and felt better about
themselves when they used the Internet. The social
compensation hypothesis is the second.

The social compensation hypothesis according to
Desjarlais and Willoughby (2010) suggests that some
socially anxious individuals report that compensating
for their social anxiety is a reason they use computers with friends, particularly online communication.
Under this hypothesis teenagers attempt to compensate for weak social skills by seeking attention on
the Internet where fewer social skills are required.
In contrast to extroverts, introverts showed declines
in well being associated with these same variables.
The theory implies that the Internet satisfies emotional
needs more so for extroverted teens than for introverted teens.

Because of reduced auditory and visual cues and
anonymity, introverted teens may compensate for
their shyness by using the Internet (Peter et al., 2005).
Introverted teens may be unable to respond effectively
to cues such as body language or facial expressions

and find it easier to communicate online where these cues play a lesser role (Peter et al., 2005). Introverted teens using the Internet may communicate better without having to respond to actual conversation and meeting individuals face to face (Peter et al., 2005).

The Internet may support and enhance the weak social skills of introverted teens. Based on the social compensation hypothesis introverted individuals may easily self-disclose personal information online that may facilitate the formation of online friendships (Lee, 2009). Introverted teens may try to compensate for their lack of social skills by using the Internet. The Internet may serve as a substitute for lack of a social network offline because socially anxious people may feel more at an advantage in developing intimate relationships online (Lee, 2009).

Introverted teens that feel uncomfortable with establishing relationships in person, may feel more comfortable with establishing relationships online (Lee, 2009). Internet predators can take advantage of introverted teens which are more willing to post personal information on social websites such as Facebook®, MySpace™ and Twitter©.

Problematic Account

General Problem. "Some news reports have suggested that law enforcement is facing an epidemic of these [child molestation] sex crimes perpetrated through a new medium [the Internet] by a new type of criminal," (Wolak et al., 2008, p. 2). The rise of the Internet has led to a new wave of child molestation, caused by a new type of criminal, the Internet predator. Given adequate information, law enforcement may be able to prevent this epidemic from deepening.

Specific Problem. Youth in this Midwestern United States town High School are establishing dangerous relationships online with people whom they have never met. According to News 4, KVOA.com (2012) a Massachusetts youth volunteer has been arraigned after a boy told local authorities that he was enticed into sexual acts by the man as they chatted over an Internet web cam. Chat rooms and online social websites are places where in a recent survey, 25% of youth in the United States reported that they established online friendships with strangers (Peter et al., 2005). A group of Midwestern United States town, teachers and counselors were asked open-ended qualitative questions to help discover causes and possible solutions to this phenomenon.

Commitment

This guide is committed to exploring the perceptions that teachers/counselors have of the issues involved with 13 to 17 year old teenagers falling victim to child predators on the Internet and it was designed to obtain knowledge by allowing teachers/counselors to answer open ended interview questions about their opinions on the lived Internet sexual assault experiences of teenagers. Its commitment was also to find ways that may help reduce the number of sex offenses against teenagers by someone whom he or she met on the Internet. The opinions of teachers and counselors are used to help reduce the number of Internet sexual assaults.

The guide involves the interviewing of 25 Midwestern United States town High Schoolteachers/counselors who have worked with teenaged Internet sexual assault victims about their opinion on teen Internet sexual assault causes and possible solutions. This research explored the social needs, which teenagers are fulfilling on the Internet, and how those needs could be met without exposing the teenagers to Internet predators. The guide may add to the amount of information available to educators, parents, mental health professionals and law enforcement about the Internet teen rape phenomenon in the Midwestern United States town area.

This Midwestern United States town has a population of one million; there are 25 middle and high schools in the area and 1000 teachers/counselors residing within the Midwestern United States town. Using qualitative research methods including open-ended interview questions was an appropriate research method for uncovering the participants' opinions about some of the causes of Internet sexual offenses among teenagers. This guide may provide insight to educators, parents, mental health professionals and law enforcement to help teenagers avoid encountering child predators on the Internet. These teachers/ counselors have opinions that may lead to insight into how teenagers fall victim to Internet predators and how to prevent the assault.

Implication

General Importance. University of New Hampshire researchers showed that in one year, one fifth of the people using chat rooms and social networking sites were asked to engage in sexual activity (Grenada, 2008). These solicitations, if accepted by teens, could lead to sexual exploitation or rape. The importance of this guide is that it may provide educators, parents, mental health professionals and law enforcement information on the teen online sexual offense phenomenon, on which to develop laws, to build curriculum and to develop parenting strategies.

Unlike previous studies of teenage online sexual assault this guide focused on teen needs and behavior on the Internet, and how those needs and behaviors increase the likelihood of encounters with predators. Previous studies like the McCarthy (2010) study explored the Internet sexual activity of two groups of adult male child pornography offenders, this guide sought to identify potential risk factors associated with those offenders who also sexually abused minors. Also the Bagwell (2009) study, which is entitled "Trends in Arrests of 'Online Predators,'" found that arrests of Internet predators stalking children rose by 400% between 2000 and 2006. These studies do not address the role that teen behavior plays in the teen Internet sexual assault phenomenon.

Leadership Importance. Leaders of law enforcement organizations and secondary education institutions may be able to use the data collected in this research to establish or improve upon Internet rape prevention curriculum. Because they are likely to see the results in increased teen drug use, alcoholism or in decreased academic performance, mental health practitioners need an accurate assessment of the nature and prevalence of this new teen Internet sexual assault phenomenon (Wolak et al., 2008). Mental health professionals can then also assist parents in educating their teens. Finally, this guide may also be significant because it provides parents with information that they can use to discuss with their teenager; how to prevent online sexual assault.

Inquiry Environment

This guide evaluates the interview responses of 25 teachers/counselors in Midwestern United States town who have worked with teens that have experienced a sexual relationship with someone whom they met on the Internet. The purpose of the interviews was to ask open-ended questions concerning the causes of teen Internet sexual assault among 13 to 17 year-olds. The guide evaluates the responses to the question of which type of student he or she believes would most likely be rape victims following initial contact on the Internet. Finally the interviewees were asked their opinion on potential solutions to the teen Internet sexual assault problem.

A qualitative research method that uses open-ended research questions to collect data about the teen Internet sexual assault phenomenon is more appropriate than the quantitative or mixed research methods. The qualitative method provides for the collection of a variety of opinions from adults who interact with teenagers daily. The qualitative research method used in this guide will also provide for the ranking of responses to interview questions, and to the determination of which teen needs or behavior will most likely result in contact with Internet predators.

Finally, using the qualitative research method will help to determine which solutions to teen Internet sexual assault are most useful in the opinion of the interviewees. The qualitative, open-ended questions given to the interviewees helped to form a picture of the teenager's motivation for seeking companionship on the Internet. The questions helped to provide insight into the question of which teens are likely to fall victim to predators. The qualitative method uncovered techniques that may result in the prevention of teenage Internet assault.

Investigative Inquiry

The primary research question was; what are the perceptions of teachers/counselors concerning the causes of the teen Internet sexual assault phenomenon. The following questions were secondary research questions. What are the perceptions of teachers/counselors concerning the following questions? What role does teen needs play in the teen Internet sexual assault phenomenon; needs such as identity, companionship and sex? Are social networking websites relevant in teen Internet sexual assault? What measures could possibly reduce the phenomenon; for example, education, parenting and law enforcement?

The teachers/counselors participating in the guide were asked a set of interview questions. To determine which type of teenager is most likely to fall victim to an Internet predator, they were asked the following questions.

1. Please share with me your opinion on what circumstances most likely lead to teenage sexual encounters with someone whom they meet on the Internet?
2. Please share with me your opinion on how teenagers will most likely meet people on the Internet; for example, in a chat room, on MySpace™, on Facebook® or something totally different?
3. What role do you feel that a teen's personality;

(for example, introverted, extraverted, or something totally different plays in whether they will meet a predator on the Internet?

   a. Do you feel that an introverted teen is more likely to attract a predator?

   b. Do you feel that an extroverted teen is more likely to attract a predator?

4. Please share with me your opinion on the role that teen gratification; for example, sex, companionship, self –esteem, or something else plays in whether a teen will meet an Internet predator?

5. Demographic data

   a. Sex (male or female)

   b. Number of children

   c. Ethnicity

Finally, to seek possible solutions to the problem, the interviewees were asked to please share with me your opinion on what support would most likely help; for example, more parental supervision, better law enforcement, better High School curriculum or other to prevent teen's contact with an Internet predator and would it be okay to contact them if there are follow on questions?

Outline of the Intangibles

Broad Intangible Area. The broad theoretical area that this research deals with is social change or a paradigm shifts among teenagers caused by the Internet revolution. The Internet is creating a new global social paradigm. According to Greenfield and Zheng (2006), teen values such as whom they identify with, how they deal with sexual needs and how they increase their self-esteem are played out in chat rooms and on Facebook®, MySpace™ and Twitter©.

In the past, teens may have established their identity by cruising down Main Street on a Friday night, but they establish their identity in Internet social networking websites such as Facebook®, MySpace™ and Twitter©. Adult parents who use the Internet less than teens need to understand the risk of sexual exploitation that teens face on the Internet. Teens also use more Internet-based tools than adults such as chat rooms and instant messaging which could subject them to more contact with Internet predators. The frequency of teen Internet use and the type of tools used could be factors which influence teen Internet sexual assault.

Intangible Gap. No study has been found that examined specifically the role of teenage developmental behavior in Internet rape cases. The role that introverted or extroverted personality plays in the teen Internet assault phenomenon has not been fully explored. Interest in whether a teen is more likely or less likely to encounter a predator on the Internet based on introversion/extroversion is growing.

Expectations

Burns and Grove (2001) stated that recognizing and stating the exceptions of the study is necessary because assumptions present a potential for bias and misunderstanding, they also influence the logic of the study. An exception was that participants would understand how the confidentiality and anonymity of their responses will be maintained, and that they would answer interview questions honestly when sharing their opinion on lived experiences is also assumed. Additional assumptions included that the participants knew victims of teen Internet sexual assault as defined in this guide, and were representative of the teacher/counselor population.

A further exception was that participants have some understanding of teen gratification and needs. According to Benner (1994) in qualitative, phenomenological design studies assumptions are important because these studies engage participants; in contrast to the disengaged, participant-object approach used in quantitative research. It was assumed that the participants would understand and interpret interview questions as written. Understanding is threefold, – (a) a familiarity one has with the world, (b) a point of view one has from their background, and, lastly, (c) an expectation about the interpretation (Benner, 1994).

According to Shank (2002), while recognizing that there are many realities; phenomenological studies must be designed to take into consideration "personal" assumptions regarding reality (p. 95). Finally, I assumed that the participants understood what social networking websites and chat rooms were. I also assumed that the participants understood basic needs such as the need for attention, companionship and sex. An exception was also made that the participants could recognize teenage introverted and extroverted personality.

Opportunity

The opportunities that lie in this of the guide will add to a growing body of literature about the teen Internet sexual assault and ways to help prevent the phenomenon. The sample focused on teachers/counselors who have worked with teenagers who were sexually assaulted by someone whom they met on the Internet. The body of knowledge on teen Internet assault risk factors and the importance of parental, educational and law enforcement support in preventing this phenomenon form the opportunities for this research. A phenomenological exploration of teen personality types which are more likely to lead to encounters with predators on the Internet and the type of measures which are likely to prevent these encounters will add insight about ways to help protect teens while they use the Internet.

Constraints

Guide participants were not selected randomly, which is a limitation. Phenomenology seeks only individuals who are willing to describe their experiences about the phenomenon being studied (Burns & Grove, 2001). A further limitation was that only teachers/counselors who were willing to volunteer their opinion on teen Internet sexual assault causes were contacted about the guide; those unwillingly to participate will not be contacted. Gilgun (2005) noted problems associated with qualitative research include "generalizability, subjectivity and language" (p. 40); those difficulties could have occurred in this guide and were recognized. The geographic area in which the study was conducted constrains the outcomes because of the unique law enforcement, mental health and educational programs available in this Midwestern United States town area may not be available in other locations.

Participants could stop the interview at any time in which case the participant's information would not be included with the guide. Subjectivity is minimized during the interview by remaining objective with participant information and following the modified Van Kaam method. Using the modified Van Kaam method and remaining objective with participant information will help reduce subjectivity limitations. Finally, the male researcher interviewed both male and female participants.

Delineations

According to Critchlow (2005), scope by listing what is not included or intended in the study. A delineation of the guide was that information about specific social support persons, services or agencies was not intended to be evaluative or accurate reflections of programs; rather the information was shared as a descriptive, personal report of the participants' view. A second delineation was that the guide does not portend to provide exhaustive or quantitative data about characteristics of teenagers or social needs, particularly of teenaged Internet sexual assault victims.

Definition of Terms

Introverted. Introverted is defined as a person's tendency to prefer his or her own company to large social events and quiet reflection to social interaction (Peter et al., 2005).

Extroverted. Extroverted refers to a person's inclination to seek company and social interaction (Peter et al., 2005).

Rich-Get-Richer Hypothesis. The rich-get-richer hypothesis states that the Internet will primarily benefit extroverted individuals. Because contact can be made more easily online, the greater social skills of extroverted individuals can develop fully and will facilitate the formation of online friendships (Peter et al., 2005).

Social Compensation Hypothesis. Social compensation hypothesis states that because of reduced auditory and visual cues and anonymity, the Internet may enable introverted people to compensate for their weaker social skills (Peter et al., 2005).

Sexual Solicitations and Approaches. Sexual solicitations and approaches includes requests to engage in sexual activities or sexual talk or give personal sexual information unwanted or whether wanted or not, made by an adult (Taylor, Caeti, Loper, Fritsch & Liederbach, 2006).

Aggressive Sexual Solicitation. Aggressive sexual solicitation includes sexual solicitations involving offline contact with the perpetrator through regular mail, by telephone, or in person or attempts for requests for offline contact (Taylor et al., 2006).

Harassment. Harassment is the threat or other offensive behavior (not sexual solicitation) sent online to the youth or posted online about the youth for others to. Not all such incidents were distressing to the youth who experienced them (Taylor et al., 2006).

Distressing Incidents. Distressing incidents were episodes that youth rated themselves as very or extremely upset or afraid as a result of the incident (Taylor et al., 2006).

Cyber abuse. Cyber abuse is a term that encompasses a wide range of aggressive online activities, including bullying, stalking, sexual solicitation and pornography (Mishna, McLuckie & Saini, 2009).

Child sex tourism. The United Nations (UN) defines child sex tourism (CST) as organized tourism (the nature of which encompasses many activities) that facilitates the commercial sexual exploitation of anyone under 18 years of age (Patterson, 2007).

Summary

Review

Teenage Internet rape is a negative outgrowth of the Internet revolution. Yet, there is very little research regarding the effects of teenage development in this phenomenon. This research is used to examine the role that teenage development plays in Internet teenage rape cases. Research findings may be important for school leaders and law enforcement leaders for developing curriculum that will assist in the prevention of teenage Internet rape.

The research included interviews with 25 teachers/counselors in a Midwestern United States town who have worked with teens that experienced a sexual relationship with someone who they met on the Internet. The interviews consisted of open-ended questions involving potential causes of the phenomenon, most likely victims and potential ways to reduce the problem of teenage Internet rape. Chapter 2 is a review of recent literature covering teen Internet sexual assault. The review further covered literature on (a) the role of teen behavior, (b) role of the ages of the teen and the predator, (c) social networking sites and (d) the teen Internet sex phenomenon knowledge gap.

Current Literature

THE CURRENT LITERATURE covers current literature on the teen Internet assault phenomenon. To provide a comprehensive overview of the current literature; the chapter presents an orderly, logical and flowing presentation of the research material published on the teen Internet assault phenomenon. This chapter also includes material that is germane to the research question of how teen Internet behavior may contribute to the likelihood of encounters with predators on the Internet.

A historical overview of the literature that has outlined the Internet teen sexual assault phenomenon is also included. This chapter covers material that outlines the role of introversive and extroversive teen personalities in Internet teen assaults. A general discussion on teen personalities and how their behavior contributes to the likelihood of encountering a predator on the Internet is also covered.

This chapter includes a discussion on specific Internet social networking sites and tools such as Facebook®, MySpace™, Twitter© and chat rooms and the role that they play in increasing the chance of teen contact with Internet predators. Investigation for this literature review covered eight topic areas: the international scope of teen Internet assault, increased teen Internet use, role of teen behavior, role of anonymity, role of age in teen sexual assault, teen social networking on the Internet, Internet predators and gaps in literature.

Subsections in some of the topic areas further describe issues and pertinence to the guide. Subsections under role of teen behavior are defined: gratification, introversive, and extroversive teen personalities. Subsections under role of teen behavior defined the role of age in teen sexual assault including the ages of both victim and predator. Subsections under teen social networking on the Internet outline social websites and chat rooms. Subsections under gaps in knowledge include gaps in law enforcement, education, and parenting.

Other areas outlined in the literature are important to the teen Internet assault phenomenon including child pornography and potential solutions outlined in literature. The literary review subsections are outlined in the below tree diagram.

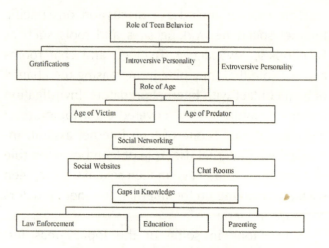

Figure 1. Literary Review Tree Diagram

The literature review included database searches in peer reviewed, professional journals on issues of Internet teen assault, Internet predators as well as current laws designed to protect children using the Internet. Further literature sources accessed included peer-reviewed articles on qualitative research and phenomenology as well as texts based on research methods, social science research, qualitative research, and social support theory texts. Finally, the chapter also compares and contrasts literature that contains two points of view on the teen Internet assault phenomenon.

One point of view focused on the teenager and shaping teenage behavior to prevent Internet sexual assault. The other point of view focused on the

Internet predator; identifying his or her behavior and steps that may be taken to prevent his or her encounter with teens.

International Scope of Teen Internet Assault

Fusilier, M. (2008) stated that the United States has the largest number of Internet users of any country in the world and that it has the second highest penetration rate after Sweden (74.3%) followed by Australia (65.4%). Internet crime is increasingbecoming an international phenomenon. According to Nair (2006) the number of people in the United Kingdom (UK) who [were] cautioned or charged over Internet child pornography quadrupled between 2001 and 2003 (Nair, 2006).

Recent research from Gartner estimates that in 2003 only 9% of mobile phones sold in Western Europe had embedded cameras (Nair, 2006). Embedded cameras are often used to take pornographic photos and upload them to the Internet. The number of embedded cameras was projected to rise to 45% in 2005 and to 66% in 2006.

Photographs could reveal personal and location details of the subject, for instance the school name or a park where the child might be visiting on a regular basis which if distributed inappropriately could reach the wrong hands of predators seeking contact with children (Nair, 2006). As the number of Internet users increase so does the number of Internet criminals who traffic child pornography. As the number of Internet criminals grows internationally, it also continues to increase in America.

Wang, Bianchi, & Raley (2005) stated that the Internet may soon rival television as the most important media outlet in American families. Similar to the television rating system which protects children under the age of 18 from harmful material, a system could be developed to protect children from the harmful effects of the Internet. The Internet presents new challenges to parents' ability to supervise their children's usage given that 64% of online teens say they know more about the Internet than their parents, and 66% of parents agree (Wang et al., 2005).

Educators, parents, mental health professionals and law enforcement need knowledge in order to assist parents in protecting children from the harmful material and criminals on the Internet. According to Gallagher (2008), reports suggest that hundreds of children are trafficked into the UK each year for the purposes of sexual exploitation. According to research in the past five years; teen Internet use and online sexual assault cross international borders (Gallagher, 2008).

The Internet allows communication to cross both national and international boundaries. Recent literature reported that Internet child sexual abuse is becoming a big problem in the United Kingdom (UK) (Gallagher, 2008). Stathopulu, Hulse and Canning

(2003) stated that community pediatricians are increasingly asked to provide expert opinion on Internet child pornography related to 'sex tourism', mostly in Southeast Asian countries.

The Internet is often used to organize child exploitation activities. For example, according to Rambaree (2008) Mauritius has an estimated 2,600 child prostitutes and is a source and destination country for children trafficked for the purpose of commercial sexual exploitation. Predators not only use the Internet to contact teens locally; they also use the Internet nationally and internationally to organize and control networks among themselves.

According to White (2004) information communication technologies such as the Internet play a particularly important role not only in the promotion and packaging of sex travel but of a new type of global surveillance of bodies, race, and desire. Not only are children exploited directly by predators on the Internet; criminals also use the Internet to organize international child exploitation rings. Threats from predators on the Internet, not only come from local or national users. Threats can come from anywhere in the world.

Increased Teen Internet Use

The Internet has grown tremendously since the 1990s. The Internet has expanded from simple web pages to include social websites such as Facebook®,

MySpace™ and Twitter©. The use of Internet communications applications including e-mail and text messaging has expanded tremendously in recent years.

Shannon (2008) found that the expansion in Internet use in the mid-1990s has created a largely unmonitored forum for contacts between adults and children. The few studies that do exist show that in 2003, 32% of a nationally representative school sample of children aged 9 - 16 reported that they had experienced someone talking about sex with them on the Internet when they did not want this (Shannon, 2008). In recent years these technologies created a new social environment on the Internet.

According to Taylor, Caeti, Loper, Fritsch, & Liederbach (2006), the use of the Internet for exploitation, stalking, and obscenity has grown substantially since 1990. Because Internet sexual assault has grown rapidly, research and data collection in this area has not kept pace. In a representative school survey of 15 year-olds conducted in 2005, the Swedish National Council for Crime Prevention found that slightly over 30% of the youth reported that they had been the subject of some form of sexual contact during the previous 12 months from an unknown person that they knew or believed to be an adult (Shannon, 2008).

As the use of the Internet grows, so does the Internet exploitation of children. According to Loughlin and Taylor-Butts (2009), growing access to technology may increase the risk of online sexual exploitation of children and youth. According to Wells and Mitchell (2007) teens are often using social networking websites and chat rooms as a way to communicate with friends, meet new people and find entertainment. Teens are more likely to contact each other through the Internet than are adults. In recent literature, Mishna, McLuckie and Saini (2009) found that information technology's role in society multiplies with each generation.

In the future, communication technology such as cell phones, social networking websites and chat rooms will play an even greater role for both teenagers and adults. Law enforcement efforts and education about crimes committed using technology could be expanded exponentially. The Internet has led to a new set of crimes that did not exist 15 years ago. Kennison (2005) stated that crimes involving the Internet were virtually unheard of 15 years ago when the start of the 1990s heralded in this new medium of communication.

With every generation, the number of individuals using the Internet grows and with it grows the number of Internet predators and Internet child pornographers. Rimington and Gast (2007) argued that the rapid growth of the Internet initiated in 1993 continues to the present-day. The Internet has broadened the horizon of youth. With the Internet, a child's experiences can go far beyond his or her community.

The child predator may be someone living next

door or someone living in the next county or state. In general, the Internet has changed communication. Gallagher (2005) argued that technology has changed drastically the way in which we communicate with one another and interact more generally. It is not unusual to communicate with someone across town, across the country or across the globe. Both professional and personal communication has changed for children and adults.

Global communications and the Internet have increased the number and types of individuals with whom children can communicate. The risk of child exposure to pornography and exploitation has increased along with the rise of the Internet. According to recent literature associated with using the Internet, sexual assault is a risk that teens face.

Chief among these are the risks children face in being made the subjects of, or exposed to pornography (and the possibility of being groomed over the Internet for child sexual abuse (CSA) (Gallagher, 2005). The global nature of the Internet also increases the child's risk of meeting a predator. Recent literature suggests that Internet exploitation of children has now caught the eye of the media. According to Wolfe & Higgins (2008) recent public and media attention has been given to the online solicitation of children for sex.

The television show *Predator Raw* on MSNBC™ is one of the programs high lighting tactics used by predators to solicit teenagers for sex. According to

The Harvard Mental Health Letter (2008), more than four out of five teens have access to a cell phone, BlackBerry, personal data assistant or computer. Internet predators can reach teens by sending instant messages to their cell phones or by sending an email or picture to their Blackberry or computer.

These Internet devices open new avenues to interact and exploit teens. According to literature, before 1990 there were sparse reports of child trafficking. Around 1990 there was very little reporting of child sex trafficking in news reports and magazine articles (O'Grady, 2001). Teen Internet sexual assault is a relatively new phenomenon.

Twenty years ago, there was very little evidence that Internet child exploitation existed. According to the CioInsight (2007), in June 2007 the police in the United Kingdom smashed a global Internet pedophile ring with 700 members and rescued more than 30 children from abuse. The Internet has become a media source used by international pedophile organizations. Pedophiles from 35 different countries were targeted by police for distributing thousands pornographic photographs of children (CioInsight, 2007).

Literature has focused on the teen or child Internet assault because teen Internet use has increased dramatically and this new phenomenon has evolved faster than society has developed ways to control it. Recent studies have stated that adolescents use on-line communications more than adults. Adolescents spend more time on the Internet and are more likely to meet individuals online than are adults. If a teen is introverted or extroverted or whether they spend time in online chat rooms or on Facebook®, MySpace™ and Twitter©, could increase the likelihood that they will meet someone either friend or foe.

Teens spend a large amount of time making friends online. According to research, whether teens are introverted or extroverted may play a role in these online friendships. Introverted teens that are unable to find relationships offline may seek them on the Internet. The Internet may also be an outlet for intro-verted teens to establish not only friendships, but also sexual relationships.

The Internet is increasingly used as an outlet for sexual activity. According to recent literature, the ac-cessibility, affordability and anonymity of the Internet make it highly appealing to users (Rimington & Gast, 2007). Teens that are seeking sexual activity online could potential fall victim to Internet predators.

Increasing time spent online for sexual activity may lead to cybersex abuse and compulsive cyber-sex behavior (Rimington & Gast, 2007). Teens can also create a number of different identities online as well as encounter many. According to recent findings, computers and the Internet affect human information exchanges.

Computers change the quality of information ex-change. Steinberg (2009) states that a geographically knowable discourse has become a spaced-out, location-free zone unbound by time, place or personal history. Internet predators can meet teens at any time and from any location while online.

Recent research discovered these information exchanges often led to online sexual solicitations. Internet predators may be less restricted by time, space and personal information about a potential victim than predators that use physical means to contact their victims. Recent literature suggested the computer and the Internet are the new frontier.

As in other frontiers, vulnerable individuals could have protection from predators. The playwright Sam Shepherd addresses the changing nature of self-reflection and expression: *The struggle with the land is finished*. Now the frontier is the computer, so it has become an internal thing (Steinberger, 2009).

The initial physical contact between predator and teen is no longer the main issue for law enforcement and parents because initial contact between predator and teen is often made online, through social websites, chat rooms or instant messaging. Law enforcement has to focus on the date that is made between the teen and the predator after initial contact is made online. This is one example of the Internet caused cultural communication transformations to which educators, parents, mental health professionals and law enforcement could adapt.

The cultural transformation of communication

affects language, social intercourse, and attitudes toward the self, significant others and the global community (Steinberger, 2009). The cultural transformation caused by the Internet has added new words or abbreviations to language, for example a best friend is now a "BF." We now text and e-mail each other instead of writing letters.

Identity for teenagers is partly determined on Facebook®, MySpace™ and Twitter© and less so during traditional events such as the senior prom. According to recent literature, the rise in teen Internet usage has played a role in the rise of sexual abuse and exploitation. According to Choo (2009), 55% of all United States teenagers between the ages of 12 and 17 years surveyed in a recent study, used social networking sites such as Facebook®, MySpace™ and Twitter©.

Chat rooms and social websites can become a means for sexual abuse and exploitation. Between 2000 and 2005, Internet usage for children ages 12 to 17 increased from 56% to 87%, predators now have access to this vulnerable population (Wells & Mitchell, 2007). In principle, the Internet sex predator could have access to approximately 55% of United States 12 to 17 year olds. Teens need assistance in protecting themselves when using this new electronic technology.

They could take precautions when using social network sites such as Facebook®, MySpace™ and

Twitter© to communicate with friends. According to Dombrowski, Gischlar, & Durst (2007), 98% of children between the ages of 11 and 19 reported using the Internet weekly to chat with friends, complete homework or as a form of entertainment. With the large number of children using the Internet, more could be known about child Internet behavior to help protect the teen from potential predators. Despite recent studies that revealed significant teen Internet use, very few educational programs exist that instruct teens on how to use the Internet safely.

In spite of the danger from predators on the Internet, safety instruction was only given to 36% of children who claimed to be regular users (Dombrowski et al., 2007). More knowledge could be gained and distributed on the teen Internet sexual assault phenomenon which curriculum can be built on to help protect children while they are on the Internet. Recent literature has also raised concerns that extensive use of the Internet could cause teens to become isolated from friends and family members (Wang et al., 2005).

Recent literature has discovered that with more than 10 million users under the age of 18 on the Internet, something could be done to protect them from predators. The Internet is becoming a new venue for sexual predators. The old street corner and playground method of meeting teens has changed for the pedophile. In a recent study, a sample of 1,501 regular Internet users, ages 10 to 17 were interviewed

(Taylor et al., 2006). The guide uncovered that some of the teens had been approached and solicited for sex on the Internet.

Studies have shown that 1 in 33 teens have received extremely heavy sexual solicitation; they have been asked to meet at places, received telephone calls, received mail, money or gifts (Taylor et al., 2006). Teens are not only solicited for sex by the traditional means they are also solicited online. Recent research has found that 25% of youths in the guide reported chat room or social networking site relationships with strangers (Peter et al., 2005). These friendships develop on sites like Facebook®, MySpace™ and Twitter©. Recent research supported the social compensations hypothesis.

Role of Teenage Behavior

Gratification. According to Greenfield and Zheng (2006) the gratifications from these communication media [the Internet] range from global leadership experience to identity and sexuality to self-injury and self-concept. Gratification is a motive or need ranging from identity and sexuality to self-injury and self-concept. Gratification plays an important role in teen development. Gratification can be positive; for example when forming identity, sexuality or leadership skills; it can also be negative, in terms of self-destructive behavior (Greenfield & Zheng, 2006). The Internet can influence teen development. An adolescent's identity can be partly constructed when the teen constructs a profile on Facebook®, MySpace™ and Twitter©. Their sexuality dynamic is partly determined by whom they meet and communicate with on these sites.

One of the key findings of uses-and-gratifications research has also proven influential for Internet research: People use the Internet for different goals and the consequences of this use vary depending on these goals (Peter et al., 2005). Not only do teens seek gratification from relationships on the Internet, but predators are also on the Internet seeking gratification. This presents the potential for teens to inadvertently chat with predators while seeking sexual gratification. The predator may try to directly to entice the teen into a sexual relationship or to seduce them for future sexual encounters. Teens become more vulnerable to Internet sexual assault when they form friendships with strangers online (Mishna et al., 2009). Teens seeking relationships on the Internet are especially vulnerable to the Internet teen predator.

Introverted Teens. Recent literature focused on two hypotheses; one is the social compensation hypothesis and the rich-get-richer hypothesis. The so-called rich-get-richer hypothesis states that the Internet will primarily benefit extraverted individuals (Peter et al., 2005). These two theories deal with the question of whether introverted or extroverted teens are more likely to encounter unhealthy relationships on the Internet while trying to fulfill their need for companionship.

According to the social compensation hypothesis, introverted people including teens will find greater satisfaction using the Internet because they can compensate for weaker social skills (Peter et al., 2005). Socially anxious youth are often less well liked than less anxious peers and tend not to be affiliated with a peer crowd and report lower levels of companionship and intimacy (Desjarlais & Willoughby, 2010). Introverted teens are more likely to form relationships on the Internet than extroverted teens (Peter et al., 2005).

Introverts will communicate more frequently online than extroverts and will consequently make more online friends than extraverts do (Peter al et al., 2005). Lack of visual cues on individuals may enhance teen fantasies of the people whom they meet on the Internet. On the Internet, visual cues are missing that could assist teens in judging who is, trustworthy and sincere and who is not.

This lack of visual cues could also lead to teens fantasizing about potential partners (Wells & Mitchell, 2007). Teens could fantasize about a same age partner whom they have met on the Internet when the partner could in fact be an adult predator. Having not seen the individuals with whom they are communicating with on the Internet, teens may fantasize about the individual with whom they are communicating. A potential predator could send fake photos and lie about their identity to entice the teen into a sexual relationship.

According to the literature, introverted teens communicate more frequently online than do extroverted teens. In principle, introverts are more likely to form online friendships. Increased teen online communications could inadvertently lead to more communications with online predators.

Extroverted Teens. The rich-get-richer hypothesis, also outlined in recent studies suggested that extroverted teens would find it easier to establish relationships on the Internet than introverted teens (Peter et al., 2005). The so-called rich-get-richer hypothesis states that the Internet will primarily benefit extroverted individuals. An extroverted teen's strong social skills could potentially draw them into relationships on the Internet. Individuals who already are comfortable in social situations may use the computer, either in person or online, to seek out additional opportunities to socialize (Desjarlais & Willoughby, 2010). They can seek gratification from knowing that they can make friends easily in chat rooms and on social networking sites.

Role of Anonymity

The anonymity of the Internet allows both the predator and victim to hide their true identity and take on the role of someone else. According to recent literature, Internet communication is immediate and anonymous. Before the Internet, the means to communicate such as magazines and newspapers were neither as immediate nor as anonymous (Contemporary Sexuality, 2002). Teens can receive instant feedback and gratification from strangers whom they meet in chat rooms. Recent studies suggest the Internet's anonymity encourages relationship building on the Internet.

Both the predator and the teen can use the Internet's anonymity to hide identity and inappropriate behavior. Given the anonymity in chat rooms and on social networking sites, the Internet predator uses it to exploit, stalk and sexually assault children. The perceived anonymity the Internet affords creates the opportunity for certain criminals to exploit, stalk, and commit sex crimes electronically (Taylor et al., 2006). The Internet predator, who feels that he or she is anonymous in chat rooms, can create an identity which they then use to exploit teens for sex. Recent literature focused on the role anonymity plays in online relationship and teen sexual assault. The anonymity provided by Internet communications creates favorable conditions for adults wishing to develop manipulative relationships with children (Shannon, 2008). Internet predators use these favorable conditions created by the anonymity in chat rooms to solicit children for sex.

Role That Age Plays

Age of Teenage Victims. Young children seem to be less vulnerable to child predators on the Internet than teenagers. Contact appears to be less widespread among younger children, but becomes increasingly common as children approach and enters their teenage years (Shannon, 2008). As children enter their teenage years, they become more vulnerable to the Internet predator. More than three-quarters of targeted youth (77 %) were age 14 or older (Taylor et al., 2006). The Internet and Internet teen sexual assault exist globally. A large number of children globally are using the Internet and the majority of teenagers use it at least once a day.

A recent study of Swedish children's media habits found that 95% of 12 to 16 year-olds use the Internet and that 54%, use the Internet every day (Shannon, 2008). This research focuses on teens because research has discovered that teens may be vulnerable when it comes to Internet sexual assault. Estimates of the number of children affected by online crime, child exploitation, abuse and other Internet-related crimes vary considerably.

One estimate puts the number of children who are prostituted in the United States between 100,000 and three million (Taylor et al., 2006). A large number of these children are prostituted over the Internet. Literature in the past five years uncovered that the majority of teens encountered inappropriate language on the Internet. Although this behavior may not lead to sexual assault, it is often language used by predators to seduce teens. A recent Time/CNN poll of 409 teenagers between the ages of 13 and 17 showed that

66% of the girls and 54% of the boys had experienced people saying offensive things to them online (Taylor et al., 2006).

Age of Predators. Finkelhor, Mitchell, and Wolak conducted the Youth Internet Safety Survey in 2000, interviewing a nationally representative sample of 1,501 youth, ages 10 to 17 which use the Internet regularly (Taylor et al., 2006). Young adults between the ages of 18 and 25 were the largest age group that solicited children for sex on the Internet. Those older than 25 years old make up only 4% (Taylor et al., 2006).

Teen Social Networking on the Internet

Social networking websites and Internet communications applications have led to a new form of social interaction. According to literature in the past five years, relationships on the Internet rely on fantasy and not on reality. The Internet creates interactive possibility that has never been able to exist before, yet fosters a "false sense of connection and intimacy exempting us from the real work required building relationships (Steinberger, 2009, p. 199)." Unsuspecting teens may gain a false sense of connection and intimacy from an Internet predator that they communicate with in chat rooms and on social networking websites. Current literature suggested that the majority of teens using social networking sites are creating profiles that could be a source of information for predators.

Social Websites. Lawmakers are aware of the dangers that children face from Internet predators on social networking websites and they are increasingly trying to address the problem. MySpace.com (MySpace™) that has 10 million users under the age of 18 has faced pressure to increase its controls and to do more to protect children from Internet predators (Internet Law, 2008). Teens may innocently sign up for social networking accounts only to learn that predators target them soon after they open an account.

Social networking websites are online locations where Internet predators can meet teens, gain their trust and entice them to meet in person for sex. Internet predators can use valuable information gained from social websites such as Facebook®, MySpace™ and Twitter© to meet and engage teens. Information such as age, hobbies, tastes and photos is valuable to the online predator. Social networking sites online profiles are readily available sources of information that predators can use for scouting teens (Wolak et al., 2008).

Chat Rooms. According to Subrahmanyam, Greenfield and Tynes (2004) the Kaiser Family Foundation survey conducted in Fall 2001, among online youth between 15 and 17 years, 71% were participating in chat rooms. Anonymous (2005) explains that young people using teenage chatrooms need to be aware that these chatrooms are targeted by older men who are predatory and manipulative. Individuals including teens can enter chat rooms without revealing their true identity.

An important feature of chat rooms is their anonymous nature (Subrahmanyam et al., 2004). The High Court in Edinburgh heard that Sharkey, 33, lured two girls to meetings and carried out serious sex attacks on them after posing [in a chat room] as a teenage boy (Anonymous, 2005). Most chat room participant do not use their real names. Although participants have first to register with a chat provider, most users probably provide only fictitious details about themselves (Subrahmanyam et al., 2004).

Users then choose a pseudo or nick name to use online. As part of the registration process, a user has to choose a screen name or nickname (also called a nick) that is visible when he/she is in a chat room (Subrahmanyam et al., 2004). Sharkey, of Grougar Road, Kilmarnock, even sent a photo of a young boy as he arranged to meet the two teenage girls (Anonymous, 2005).

Teens may become attracted to chat rooms because it is an Internet technology which allows them to socialize anonymously. The teen attraction to chat rooms might make them vulnerable to Internet predators. As online chat rooms combine peer interaction with a popular medium, they may be especially suitable for adolescent sexual exploration (Subrahmanyam et al., 2004).

The literature has focused a large amount of

attention on Internet predator behavior. Computer sex offenders frequently roam chat rooms and post sexually explicit material on the Internet to make contact with young children and teenagers (Taylor et al., 2006). Initial contact may start indirectly and lead to meetings with the teen. Chat rooms and instant messaging are also Internet communication tools that allow predator access to teens. The Internet predator may use one or both of these tools to start a dialogue or conversation with teens. Recent studies have found that in the national survey of youths ages 10 to 15 about 1 in 5 who reported electronic harassment in the previous year (The Harvard Mental Health Letter, 2008).

Internet Predators

Internet predators have used this new form of social interaction, the Internet as a new way to practice their predatory behavior. In the past adults exploited children whom they met in places such as in classrooms, on playgrounds or at family gatherings. Sex offenders who previously committed sex crimes against teenagers in person or through the use of telephone sex are currently committing these crimes with the help of the Internet.

The advent of the Internet has changed the way predators stalk children. Traditional law enforcement methods for preventing child molestation such as monitoring playgrounds are becoming increasingly less effective. The Internet has allowed individuals to communicate in ways uncommon in the past. Topics and sensitive areas that are rarely discussed in person between friends are often discussed openly on the Internet.

Teens searching for sexually explicit dialogue and conversation may choose chat rooms where this type language is used. Internet predators may also select these type chat rooms in hopes of finding teens whom they might exploit using this type language. According to Contemporary Sexuality (2002), some experts say the Internet validates people with niche interests, whether legal or not, by its ability to assemble a forum of likeminded people. In a chat room an Internet predator may attempt to justify his or her behavior by saying that everyone there is doing the same thing.

In online places such as chat rooms a large number of teens are approached for sex online. Annually, one in five youths are approached or solicited from people one encounters online for sexual relations (Wolfe & Higgins, 2008). The effects of online exploitation on a child can last for years. Sexual assault can be both physical and mental. With extensive time in front of the computer and online, a child can suffer long-term abuse from sexual predators on the Internet.

As the number of teens that fall victim to teen Internet sexual assault rises, the number of predators convicted is also rising. According to Burgess, Mahoney, Visk and Morgenbesser (2008), convicted sex offenders sentenced to prison increased from 81% in 1996 to 96% in 2006. The increase of child sexual offender sentences in 2006 that could indicate that law enforcement is starting to address this issue. Recent studies have shown that Internet predators are often individuals who hold position of authority over their victims.

The largest occupation category of Internet offenders in the reported media cases was a position of authority such as professional, teacher, clergy, and military (Burgess et al., 2008). Recent studies have suggested that predators are taking advantage of this new media, the Internet to exploit teens. Studies have shown that teens are receiving solicitation for sex from people whom they meet on the Internet. A telephone survey of [United States] Internet users ages 10 to 17 found that 13% had received some type of sexual solicitation online in the past year, with 4% receiving aggressive solicitations in which the solicitor attempted to make contact offline (The Harvard Mental Health Letter, 2008).

Studies have also shown that predators often approach teens on the Internet slowly and methodically. According to Sharpe (2009) despite the risks involved, including arrest and prosecution, Internet sexual predators continue to engage in behavior that is aimed towards a typical common goal: offline sexual contact with a minor. They spend time with teens while attempting to build close relationships with them. More aggressive predators will spend time developing close relationships with vulnerable children. Pervert Robert Sharkey groomed his victims online before he struck (Anonymous, 2005). Some Internet predators may send pornographic photos to entice them into a sexual relationship. They may also discover what the teen likes from their Facebook® or MySpace™ page and send them those items to encourage them to have sex.

The Internet predator may attempt to boost the teen's identity by showering them with kind words. They may then empathize with them on their side of family quarrels and finally they may convince the teen to meet for sex. Internet predators will try to find ways to gain a teen's trust, alienate the child from his or her family and eventually try to set up a meeting in which the child will be victimized (Taylor et al., 2006). Recent literature has uncovered that predators often enticed or lured teens into sexual encounters with photos and sexually explicit language.

Child predators may also use the Internet or instant messaging to communicate threats or promise rewards for sexual favors. Recent literature has discovered that predators often try to wear teens down with constant pressure to perform sexual acts. With the use of web cams and the posting of photos online, predators may try to entice teens to participate in sexual activity. Some were "worn down" by the constant pressure, as evidenced by a girl who stated. "I had enough of him threatening and asking me so I took my shirt off" (Mishna et al., 2009).

Predators may use pictures and text of a teen's prior sexual behavior placed on Facebook®, MySpace™ and Twitter© to coerce the teen into further sexual activity. According to DeFranco (2011), kids of all ages lack emotional maturity. They also need attention and validation. Coercion is sometimes a tactic used by the predator. Online predators appeared to readily use prior sexual acts as a means of coercing children and youths to engage in new acts (Mishna et al., 2009). Teens can become vulnerable to Internet predators by posting personal information such as using drugs. Recent discoveries show that Internet predators often try to coerce their teen victims into sexual encounters with drugs.

The children and youths wrote that after the real-life meetings, the older men often used illicit substances such as marijuana or crystal [methadone] meth to groom the youths for sexual encounters (Mishna et al., 2009). Posting of personal information on the Internet such as drug use may give predators information which they can use to entice teens into a sexual relationship. Recent studies have also uncovered some of the predator's mental characteristics.

Internet predators tend to have a below normal attitude towards child sexuality, as well as child emotional development. Federal agents warned that seemingly friendly Web sites like MySpace or

Facebook often are used by sexual predators as victim directories (Wolak et al., 2008). The Internet sexual predators fail to empathize with child abuse victims. Bates and Metcalf (2007) stated that the Internet group achieved lower scores on sexualized attitudes toward children, emotional congruence with children and empathy distortions with regard to victims of child abuse.

In some studies, the Internet predator showed some characteristics similar to other sexual predators; those characteristics were not explicitly (exclusive) to those of a sexual abuser. Although Internet predators have very little empathy for their child victims, they do not go as far as endorsing child sexual abuse. The research attempting to uncover more details about the behavior of Internet predators is continually ongoing.

The Malesky (2007) study stated that to gain a better understanding of this behavior, the online activity of 31 men who perpetrated or attempted to perpetrate contact sex offenses against minors they communicated with via the Internet, was examined. Malesky (2007) studied 31 men who perpetrated or attempted to perpetrate contact sex offenses against children they communicated with in Internet chat rooms to gain a better understanding of this behavior. Internet predators try to entice or encourage teens to eventually meet for sex. These Internet predators are willing to drive hundreds of miles to meet teens that they have met on the Internet. Pedophiles are using the Internet to arrange meetings with children and have been known to travel hundreds of miles for these meetings (Taylor et al., 2006).

The teen Internet sexual assault phenomenon differs from traditional child abuse because it is no longer committed by someone local. Predators now travel long distances and even cross state and national borders to meet their victims. Finally, recent research discovered that some online sex offenders have gone so far as to send plane tickets to children to fly across the country to meet them (Taylor et al., 2006). Stories are often in the news about Internet sexual predator and how they contact their victims. Popular television shows have highlighted the techniques used by Internet predators to entice teens into sexual relationships.

Child Pornography

According to Ashley (2008) a U.S. Department of Justice's Office of Juvenile Justice and Delinquency Prevention (OJJDP) 2006 study suggested that the crime of exploitation has shifted to the Internet. Research on exploitation could also shift its focus to electronic media, e.g., the Internet. In the past decade, the sexual offender has migrated from sexual abuse to child pornography and exploitation. This migration is primarily a result of increased use of the Internet. The main sex exploitation offense referred to

[United States] attorneys shifted from sex abuse (73%) in 1994 to child pornography (69%) in 2006 (Burgess et al., 2008).

Solutions Outlined in Literature

Law enforcement personnel, educators, mental health professionals and parents could develop new strategies to combat this new form of relationship for the child predator because according to Stanley (2001) societal and parental vigilance has not been extended vigorously to educating children about the dangers of the Internet. Law enforcement officers have lacked the knowledge and equipment to track offenders on the Internet but increasingly, national units are being established to address this problem (Stanley, 2001). A teen Internet sexual assault leadership model consisting of the aforementioned adult role members was developed in this guide to describe the interaction of these members (see *Figure 2*). Educators, parents, mental health professionals and law enforcement need realistic strategies to assist in impeding such relationships. According to Hines and Finkelhor (2007), if some young people are initiating sexual activities with adults they meet on the Internet; educators, parents, mental health professionals and law enforcement cannot be effective if they assume that all such relationships start with a predatory or criminally inclined adult.

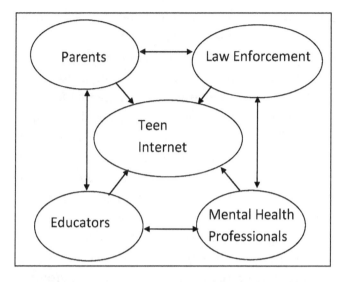

Figure 2. Teen Internet sexual assault leadership model

Current Laws

The designs of current laws protect both the teen from online assault and websites from legal liability. Current laws have stated that the owners of chat rooms and social networking sites such as Facebook®, MySpace™ and Twitter© shall not be prosecuted when Internet predators post illegal material on their websites. Although the court's holding absolved MySpace™ of legal responsibilities, its conferral of immunity under § 230 of the Communications Decency Act (CDA) effectively grants social-networking websites blanket immunity against all negligence claims (Internet Law, 2008). Internet Service Providers (ISP) are not held responsible for what users upload to their sites, but they often try to identify and report suspicious activity on their Websites.

Although most ISPs try to identify illegal activity on their sites, it is not always possible to identify a predator from someone who is conducting legal activity on a social networking site. Laws that prohibit the distribution of child pornography are also used to prevent teen sexual assault. A sexual predator can use pornography in an attempt to seduce a teen. The law prohibits the transfer of obscene material to minors, and increases penalties for offenses against children and for repeat offenders (Taylor et al., 2006).

Internet predators, who upload obscene photos and material for the purpose of soliciting sex from minors, are doing something illegal. For those that do it repeatedly, the punishment becomes increasingly steeper. Laws such as the CDA also attempt to contain the teen Internet sexual assault phenomenon by making it illegal to traffic pornographic material across state and national borders. Current laws prohibit the sending of child pornography across state and national borders. They also prohibit traveling across those borders with the intent to have sex with a child.

In 1994, the Unites States Congress extended the Mann Act by enacting the Child Sexual Abuse Prevention Act (Taylor et al., 2006). This law may assist law enforcement in catching predators that travel to meet teens who they have seduced on the Internet. This act empowers the Justice Department to penalize anyone in the United States traveling across state or national borders to engage in sexual activity with children (Taylor et al., 2006).

Although the Internet has eliminated many borders and boundaries, it is illegal for Internet predators to cross state borders to engage in sex with minors whom they have solicited for sex. The television show, *To Catch a Predator*, that exposes online predators, often uses laws that prohibit explicit sexual conversations with teens on the Internet. According to Hansen (2012) the show has volunteer experts from Perverted-Justice who pretend to be kids online. They enter Web sites like MySpace™ and Teenspot, social networking Web sites and wait to be hit on by adults looking for sex (Hansen, 2012). Those adults are then arrested by law enforcement for making harmful communications available to minors.

The Child Online Protection Act (COPA) prohibits anyone by means of a commercial website from knowingly making a communication that is "harmful to minors" available to minors under 17 for commercial purposes (Taylor et al., 2006). It is illegal to use sexually explicit language when communicating with anyone under the age of 18 in chat rooms, or on social websites such as Facebook®, MySpace™ and Twitter©. Current laws hold the producers of illegal content and not social networking sites responsible for pornographic communications with teens. Educators, parents, mental health professionals and law enforcement need additional information to better understand Internet predators and online pornographic communications.

More research is necessary to identify and prevent this type of communication. Section 230 offers two types of immunity: § 230(c) (i) stated that "no provider or user of an interactive computer service shall be treated as the publisher or speaker of any information provided by another information content provider" (Law, 2008, p. 18). According to this law ISPs that are not the actual speakers or writers of sexually explicit language are not responsible for the use of the language on their websites. Websites are not primarily responsible for preventing communications on their sites that lead to teen sexual assault. The adult that is responsible for the teen's safety is partly responsible for preventing online pornographic communications with the teen.

Educators, parents, mental health professionals and law enforcement need data to empower teens to act responsibly when interacting on these social websites. Courts have decided that social websites such as Facebook® and MySpace™ are not responsible for the prevention of adults meeting teens for sex on their websites. Recently, in Doe v. MySpace™, Inc., a United States District Court found that when MySpace™ members contacted and sexually assaulted children, MySpace™ was not liable for failing to prevent the behavior (Internet Law, 2008). Social networking websites are not responsible for illegal activity that they are unaware of but they are obligated to report activity that they uncover.

The Child Protection and Sexual Predator Punishment Act of 1998 specifically addressed the issues of online victimization of children (Taylor et al., 2006). Under this legislations, although Internet service providers are not primarily responsible for communications that may lead to teen Internet assault, they are responsible for turning over information regarding illegal acts that they uncover. This data may be used by researchers to add to the amount of information on the teen sex assault phenomenon.

ISPs can no longer ignore child pornography on their websites. The act amends the Child Abuse Act of 1990 by requiring online service providers to report evidence of child pornography offenses to law enforcement agencies (Taylor et al., 2006). Communicating on the Internet with a child using pornographic language is illegal. It is now up to law enforcement to find ways to discover and prosecute violators of these statutes. The CDA attempted to pursue that [protecting children from potentially harmful materials] interest by suppressing a large amount of speech that adults have a constitutional right to send and receive (Taylor et al., 2006). Enforcement of current laws as well as education are both tools used in the prevention of online pornographic communications and the exploitation of children on the Internet.

Contrasting Points of View

Some literature suggested that additional data and new approaches are necessary to combat this phenomenon of new teen Internet assault. This is a serious problem, but one that requires approaches different from those in current prevention messages emphasizing parental control and the dangers of divulging personal information (Wolak et al., 2008). Current literature is starting to focus on educating teens in avoiding Internet predators instead of focusing on analyzing and catching those predators. A two-pronged approach is necessary to help curb the rising number of teen Internet assault cases: one focused on arresting the predator and the other focused on educating the teen.

School courses could educate older teens about the negative effects and criminality of having sex with adults, while teaching younger teens how to be alert for and how to avoid sexual predators (Wolak et al., 2008). In the point of view of some researchers, more attention could be paid to the teen, especially at risk teens rather than to the predator. Teens could undergo risk assessments to see if they could potentially fall victim to a child predator.

Higher risk teens, those that have been sexually abused in the past, those with sexual identity issues and those that are known to have taken risk, could be given added attention (Wolak et al., 2008). Educators, parents, mental health professionals and law enforcement could have knowledge of these at risk groups in order to properly diagnose and treat teen Internet sexual assault victims. Research has also investigated the link between child pornography and molestation on the Internet.

Current research focuses more attention on the offenses and offenders than the victims. Researchers could also explore the role of teen behavior in the teen Internet sexual assault phenomenon. Effective prevention, enforcement and investigation of the offenses described here necessitate a more complete understanding of the etiology of the offenses and offenders described (Taylor et al., 2006). A combined effort focused on the victims of teen Internet assault as well as the predator is necessary.

Gaps in Literature

Researchers need to conduct more studies on teen online sex exploitation to better understand the teen Internet sexual assault phenomenon. This finding demonstrated the need for continued research in the area of online solicitation of children for sex (OSCS) (Wolfe & Higgins, 2008). According to recent literature, the high number of children who fall victim to online exploitation every year warrants further research in this area.

The growing number of OSCS victims tells us that teen Internet sexual assault phenomenon is a global problem that warrants further study. More than

750,000 children worldwide fall victim to some form of OSCS each year. These rates are indicative of an emerging societal problem worthy of further research attention (Wolfe & Higgins, 2008). Because this is a global problem, teen Internet sexual assault could be treated as a global issue and research could be geared from a global perspective.

Gaps in Educator and Parenting Knowledge. Because the Internet and teen Internet sexual assault is a new phenomenon, there is not an abundance of information and data on the subject especially from the teen's perspective. The lack of information causes a lack of understanding of the phenomenon and may slow down efforts to educate teens and the public as a whole. Educators need an accurate assessment of the nature of online child molestation to build effective education and prevention strategies. Mental health professionals may find the effects of teen Internet sexual assault in school performance and social isolation among teens. The current literature does not go far enough in decreasing fear and increasing accurate information about the teen Internet sexual assault phenomenon.

Gaps in Law Enforcement Knowledge. Law Enforcement Agencies in the United States are attempting to crackdown on child pornographers. According to Cordner (2012) a bill aiming to crackdown on child pornographers headed to the United States House of Representatives floor in February

2012. The Department of Justice is beginning to send out warnings that attempt to inform citizens that posting personal information in chat rooms and on social websites can lead to teen Internet sexual assault. According to the huffingtonpost.com (2011) on February 17, 2011, in an effort to crack down on child pornography, the Department of Homeland Security (DHS) and Department of Justice (DOJ) announced the seizure of 10 [Internet pornography] domains.

Given the proper information and knowledge, law enforcement can work to prevent this epidemic before it worsens but according to Kaelin (2012) a new tactic of concealing child porn images on legitimate looking websites poses challenges for law enforcement agencies. Law enforcement will need new tactics and techniques in order to deal effectively with sex offenders that use the Internet to perpetrate their crimes.

The explosion of pornography, exploitation attempts and crimes facilitated by the Internet has caught politicians and law enforcement completely off guard (Taylor et al., 2006). Although some research has been done on the rich-get-richer and the social compensation hypothesis, the research could go further to give more information to educators, parents, mental health professionals and law enforcement. Currently, there is no central repository for teen Internet assault data. This research will add data that law enforcement can store centrally and use to fight the phenomenon. To date, there is no central clearinghouse for the collection of data on the numbers of these types of victimizations (Taylor et al., 2006).

Conclusion

The literature discovered that teens make up the greatest number of users on the Internet. They use social networking tools like Facebook®, MySpace™, e-mail, Twitter© and instant messaging that could lead to contact with predators. Teenage girls use the Internet slightly more than boys. A teen's introverted or extroverted personality plays a role in forming relationships on the Internet. Anonymity also plays a role both for the teen and the predator in terms of contact and Internet exploitation. The literature contains gaps concerning teen behavior on the Internet; most literature is focuses on the predator. The literature also stated that law enforcement is currently slow in responding to the new Internet teen sex assault phenomenon. Current laws try to protect teens while protecting ISP) from liability and also the right to privacy.

Summary

Chapter 2 provided an historical overview of teen Internet usage both nationally and globally. It also discussed current discoveries on teen and predator Internet behavior and the role that behavior may contribute to teen Internet assaults. The chapter covered the role of introverted versus extroverted teen behavior and how one or the other could play a role in potential assaults. Chapter 2 also covered age and gender statistics of teens and adult predators that use the Internet. The chapter outlined specific laws that attempt to protect teens from an assault, and ISPs from liability. Chapter 3 explains the research methods used in this guide.

Research Methods

THE PURPOSE OF this guide is to explore teacher and counselors perceptions of the causes of 13 to 17 year-old teenagers falling victim to child predators on the Internet. Its purpose was also to find ways to help reduce the number of sex offenses against Internet users between the ages of 13 and 17, committed by someone whom he or she meets on the Internet. Chapter 3 introduces the research methods and design used in the guide. It discusses the appropriateness of using a qualitative approach in this guide that is designed to better understand teen Internet assault.

The chapter covers the interviewee sample of 25 teachers/counselors from a Midwestern United States town High School, who have worked with teens that have experienced sexual contact with someone whom they meet over the Internet. This chapter also covers data collection and rationale for the research design used in the guide. Internal and external validities of the guide are addressed in this chapter. The data analysis procedures are addressed here. This chapter also covers the guide's organization, and how it achieved maximum clarity and logical flow. Additionally, it explains ethical matters in research including the procedure for informed consent, confidentiality, and validity checks. Finally, the chapter reviews reliability and validity issues for qualitative and phenomenological research.

Appropriateness of Research Method

The exact roles of variables affecting teen Internet sexual assault are unknown. According to Creswell (2008) qualitative research is best suited for research problems in which the researcher does not know the variables and needs to further explore. From the teen behavior perspective, there is not enough literature on the teen Internet sexual assault phenomenon. The literature yields little information about the phenomenon of study and the researcher needs to learn more from participants through exploration (Creswell, 2008). There is very little literature on the teen Internet sexual assault phenomenon from the teacher/counselor's perspective. Researchers need to explore the phenomenon from the perspective of the teen victims.

Qualitative research seeks to explore and understand a central phenomenon, using interviews, and possibly observations, images or transcripts with a small number of individuals or sites (Creswell, 2008).

Quantitative research tends to address research problems requiring a description of trends or an explanation of the relationship among variables. Because teen Internet assault is a unique circumstance of the teenage experience, those victims who have lived the experience are the most knowledgeable to provide information through interviews, about which teenage behavior may contribute to the teen Internet assault phenomenon. Quantitative research methods are useful when determining trends and describing relationship variables (Creswell, 2008).

This guide is used to identify trends and relationships in the educator's responses, as he or she relate to the teen Internet assault phenomenon. The qualitative method is appropriate because the teen Internet assault phenomenon is the key concept of the study. A central phenomenon is the key concept, idea or process studied in qualitative research (Creswell, 2002). A phenomenological design enabled the exploration of how teens build inappropriate relationships on the Internet, how those relationships evolve and what factors influence the building of those relationships on the Internet.

The design of the guide is not to validate the variables that may lead to teen Internet assault. The guide design is to explore potential variables. Some quantitative research problems require that the researcher explain how one variable affects another (Creswell, 2008). The current literature on the teen Internet assault phenomenon does not outline the variables that are critical and which are less relevant to the phenomenon. Quantitative research involves studies, in which the variables are known. Not enough is known about the teen Internet assault phenomenon from the victim's perspective. Greater knowledge is gained through interviews with victims whom have lived the experience.

The literature may yield little information about the phenomenon of study, and you [the researcher] need to learn more from participants through exploration (Creswell, 2008). The guide seeks to learn from the young adult interviewees about the causes of the teen Internet sexual assault phenomenon by exploring his or her experiences. This guide attempts to explore the role of potential variables, for example, introversive and extroversive personality on the teen Internet sexual assault phenomenon. In qualitative research, the purpose is much more open-ended than in quantitative research (Creswell, 2008).

The qualitative research method used in this study on teen Internet sexual assault is appropriate because the data collected will add to the information available to educators, parents, mental health professionals and law enforcement for decision-making. In the future, these decisions could help protect teens from Internet predators. The qualitative responses from the interview sample will broaden the literature and could uncover new paradigms for combating the new teen Internet sexual assault phenomenon.

Little is known about the teen Internet sexual assault phenomenon that has evolved in the past ten years. Qualitative, phenomenological research tends to address research problems requiring a detailed understanding of a central phenomenon (Creswell, 2008). This qualitative, phenomenological study was designed to provide greater detail of teen Internet sexual assault for educators, parents, mental health professionals and law enforcement. Teens that have experienced sexual contact with someone whom they met on the Internet can provide unique insight into the phenomenon.

A qualitative, [phenomenological] research study was needed to explore this phenomenon from the perspective (Creswell, 2008) of the teen. The participants were encouraged to relay to the researcher during the interview what they feel are major contributing factors to the phenomenon. To answer the research questions on factors affecting teen Internet assault, the interviewer considered how those factors affect teenagers. The qualitative research method was appropriate for this guide because it examined teenage behavior and teenage social interaction on the Internet.

According to Salkind (2003), the purpose of qualitative study is to examine human behavior and the social, cultural, and political contexts within which it occurs. In this guide on the teen Internet sexual assault phenomenon, social and behavioral factors such as social websites and introversion/extroversion were explored. Through interview questions, the guide explored different factors that play a role in the teen Internet assault phenomenon. Because the role of different factors affecting teen Internet sexual assault is unknown, the researcher could ask different type questions.

Types of qualitative research designs include grounded theory, case study, ethnography, historical research, narrative research designs, critical social theory, and phenomenology (Burns & Grove, 2001; Creswell, 2002; Moustakas, 1994; Simon, 2006). Grounded theory seeks to unravel the elements of an experience (Moustakas, 1994) allowing the theory to be *grounded* in the data from which it arises as the researcher maintains a constant comparative process with each piece of data comparing it with other data that is obtained (Burns & Grove, 2001). The purpose of grounded theory is to build theory based on evidence from micro-level events that can be more generalized across social situations (Neuman, 2003). However, theory building was not the purpose of this guide as the intent of this study is to explore the teacher/counselor perspective on teen Internet sexual assault.

A case study design in qualitative research focuses intensely on one unit, which may be an individual, group, organization, event, or geographic unit, used to illustrate and analyze an issue (Neuman, 2003). Case studies are also helpful in demonstrating effective therapeutic techniques or generating new hypotheses (Burns & Grove, 2001). Yet, the purpose of this study was to understand the phenomena of teen Internet sexual assault and the teacher/counselor perspective on how to prevent it, with a focus on developing a deeper understanding of the meaning and nature of their everyday experiences (van Manen, 1990).

An ethnographic research design seeks to describe, analyze, and interpret a group culture of shared patterns of behavior, beliefs, and language (Creswell, 2002). Although culture, behavior, beliefs, and language may appear to influence teen Internet sexual assault, this crime goes beyond those influences and would not correspond to an ethnographic inquiry. Because of the broad diversity of teen Internet sexual assault; beliefs, language, and values this investigation would not lend itself to verification of cultural patterns as expected of an ethnographic study.

The research design chosen for this study was phenomenology because "there is not a single reality" and the purpose of the study was to explore and describe the participants' lived experiences (Simon, 2006, p. 48). Aspects of a phenomenological study may focus on (a) the participant's lived space, known as spatiality, (b) their lived body, known as corporeality, (c) lived time, known as temporality, or (d) their lived human relationships with others, known as relationality (Simon, 2006). This study aligned with the phenomena of relationality because it sought to explore the teacher/counselor perspective on the teen Internet sexual assault.

Appropriateness of Research Design

The design is appropriate because the interviews are with teachers/counselors who have worked with teenagers that have lived experience and personal knowledge of the teen Internet assault phenomenon. The responses to the interview questions will form the study's raw or primary data. This is done through a variety of tools such as interviews, historical methods, case studies and ethnography, and usually results in qualitative (or non-numeric) primary data (Salkind, 2003). The interview was an appropriate design method for this study because it gathers knowledge from individuals whom have actually lived the teen Internet sexual assault experience. The study was designed to explore the factors affecting the teen Internet sexual assault phenomenon. The study was also designed to uncover and expand on factors that contribute to the phenomenon, for example, increased teen Internet use or the use of anonymity on the Internet.

Population

The study's population consists of teachers/counselors who have worked with teenagers that have experienced a sexual relationship with someone whom he or she met on the Internet. A sample group of 25 teachers/counselors will represent the larger group of teachers/counselors who have worked with teens who have lived through teen Internet sexual assault experiences. By interviewing a sample group of teacher/counselors, this study describes trends in a large population of individuals (Creswell, 2008). The larger population consists of teachers/counselors who have worked with teens who have fallen victim to Internet sexual assault.

Sampling

Purposive sampling was used in this study because the research questions required that the sample meet certain criteria. Those criteria consisted of teachers/counselors who have worked with teenaged Internet sexual assault victims. According to Huck, Beavers and Esquivel (2010) in certain studies, the nature of the research questions necessitates that certain criteria be used to determine who or what goes into the sample.

The data was collected from the teachers/counselors who met the study's criteria. If data are collected from a group of individuals who possess these specific characteristics then that group of individuals is a purposive sample (Huck et al., 2010). The sample consists of 25 teachers/counselors in a School District in a Midwestern United States town who stated that they had worked with a teenager who has had one or more sexual experiences with someone they met on the Internet.

The teacher/counselor's responses provided a source of opinion on the teen Internet assault phenomenon. The teachers/counselors were provided informed consent forms before starting interviews (see Appendix C). The study maintained interview responses with strict confidentiality. To increase external validity, the study included both male and female participants.

To explore any ethnic anomalies, the sample also consisted of members from White, Black, Hispanic and Pacific Islander ethnic groups. The study discovered no differences among the responses from the different ethnic groups. The study could not include every teacher/counselor; it was important that the study's sample represented the general teacher/counselor population that interacts with teen Internet sexual assault victims.

When a study cannot include an entire population, then the only other choice is to select a sample subset of that population. This study could not include the entire population of United States high school teachers and counselors. The selected group of teachers/counselors from a Midwestern United States town high school was a representative sample of the teacher/counselor population who has worked with teenaged victims of Internet sexual assault.

Memory Bias

According to Windmann and Chmielewski (2008) emotionally laden events are often recalled in great detail and with high subjective confidence when they are actually inconsistent and inaccurate. The research observed key words or patterns during the interview which may identify memory bias. This discrepancy has been demonstrated in reports surrounding the terrorist attacks of 9/11/2001 and the O. J. Simpson trial. This research is cognizant of memory bias caused by the emotional nature of teen Internet assault. Open-ended clarification questions were asked in areas that may contain memory bias in an attempt to help the interviewee recall accurate events associated with their old counseling experience.

A memory bias may be caused by the emotional nature of teen Internet assault. A sample group can also supply more accurate information on a more recent event compared to a less recent event. The participants may remember their experience as old and familiar when in reality they remember less about the experience. A number of laboratory studies on the effects of emotion on memory performance have indeed found an enhanced bias to judge emotional items as familiar ("old"), whether these items are in fact old or new (Windmann & Chmielewski, 2008).

Geographic Location

The geographic location of the study was a High School Campus in a Midwestern United States town. This guide uses a field environment for the participant's interview, with settings in an environment in which the teachers/counselors relate their counseling experiences. The high school atmosphere helped to reinforce the recent experiences of the teen Internet sexual assault nature and intent of the interviews.

Informed Consent

Informed consent is an ethical principle of social research, particularly when working with vulnerable populations, and this guide followed the Belmont Report principles as outlined by the National Institutes of Health (1979). The informed consent acknowledged: (a) the purpose of the study; (b) the procedure - a personal interview with participant approval for audio-taping; (c) any risks or benefits to the participant from participating in the research; (d) a statement that their delineation participation was voluntary; (e) that all transcription and contact information was confidential, with study information kept in a secure, locked file available only to the researcher, with only an assigned letter (A to W) used as identification for the interview transcript; (f) that the participant could choose to stop participation in the research at any time without repercussions and (g) the researcher was a mandated reporter, and required to report suspected abuse or neglect of a child (see Appendix B). The study was approved by the University of Phoenix Institutional Review Board (IRB).

Pilot Study

The guide contained a pilot study designed to: (a) validate the research questions, (b) to ensure that the questions are in an effective sequence and (c) to iden-tify any research questions which need clarification. Research questions were reviewed with each partici-pant prior to signing the informed consent. A subsam-ple of five participants, two male and three female were asked to participate in the pilot study.

The five pilot study participants were not eligible to take part in the main study. During the pilot study the participants were asked about the sequencing of the questions, any needed clarifications and about aptness of the research questions after the interviews. Feedback from the pilot participants indicated no fur-ther clarification or modifications were necessary, and no requests for changes were made.

Data Collection

The teacher/counselor participants were initially contacted with authorization from the school district and school principal. The principal gave the research-er was given a list of teachers and counselors em-ployed at the school. The researcher then contacted each of the teachers and counselors and asked each of them if they had worked with teen (13-17 year olds) Internet sexual assault victims. Thirty of the teachers/counselors who had worked with those teens agreed to participate in a 10 to 15 minute open-ended, semi-structured interview about their perspective on teen Internet sexual assault, see interview protocols (Appendix D). The researcher then scheduled the interviews at the date, time and location on the school campus of the teacher/counselor's choosing.

The interviews were conducted at the agreed upon time and place using a semi-structured interview. The participants were read and reviewed the informed consent statement, noting any risks of discomfort in personal sharing or distress in reflecting on individual concerns. The qualitative open-ended question design does not measure teen Internet assault variables, but instead explores potential causes of the phenomenon. In qualitative research, data collection is not begun with a pre-established instrument to measure distinct variables (Creswell, 2008). The interview protocols (see Appendix D) included data collection forms that outlined the interview.

The researcher in this guide learned from the participants in the study and developed forms called protocols for recording data as the guide proceeded. The guide's protocols contained questions about teen Internet sexual assault that focused the interviewee's attention to factors that were associated with the phenomenon. Although the interviews started with open-ended questions, often the questions on these forms changed and emerged during data collection (Creswell, 2008). Interviewee responses to questions were gathered for later analysis. Transcribed audio recordings formed a database composed of frequently words.

Data collection involved asking the teachers/

counselors open-ended questions that required more than yes or no answers. The purpose of these questions was to record their opinions on factors that affect teen Internet assault. This form contains general questions so the constituents could provide their own responses to the questions (Creswell, 2008).

To document and understand age, gender and race of the interviewees, the study data collection forms also contained demographic questions. The data collection form consisted of the open-ended interview questions as well as space for follow on questions. According to Marczyk, DeMatteo and Festinger (2005), when researchers collect data, their first step is to develop a data collection form.

Because the questions in this guide were open-ended, responses and raw data were open-ended and wide ranging. Similar to a jigsaw puzzle, unorganized responses to interview questions, on personality, websites and behavior were placed in an organized manner. The guide extensively explored the interviewee's opinions on the teen Internet sexual assault phenomenon, through the use of the open-ended questions.

Each interview fully explored the phenomenon and included follow up questions in areas that are pertinent to the interview. The interview question design encouraged interviewees to expand on questions asked during the interview. The interviewees in this guide were encouraged to give their open and honest opinion about their teen Internet assault experiences.

Interviewees were encouraged to include additional information with their responses. This information was included in the analysis. Making the interview questions clear, concise and understandable helped to ensure the collection of the intended data. The guide also took into consideration any additional information uncovered inside or outside of the interviews that may increase knowledge on this phenomenon. Information that was not the result of an interview question but was relevant to this guide's analysis was included in the data analysis.

Validity – Internal and External

According to Cho and Trent (2006) validity in qualitative research involves determining the degree to which researchers' claims about knowledge correspond to the reality (or research participants' constructions of reality) being studied. This guide considered two types of validity, external and internal. External validity or the transferability of the rich, deep and new meaningful results to teachers and counselors was considered more important than internal validity or cause and effect.

According to Pearson, Parkin and Coomber (2011) contextualized qualitative findings can enable the transferability of qualitative research findings. The guide was designed to gather the opinions of teachers/counselors who have worked with teenagers that lived teen Internet sexual assault experiences. These results potentially may have transferability to other teachers/ counselors who have worked with teen Internet sexual assault victims.

The results of this guide were subjected to the interpretation of the researcher and the participant. Validity should not be synonymous with absolute certainty; all knowledge is differential as it is acquired via subjective interpretation (Pearson et al., 2011). By formulating questions about the research, the rigor of qualitative research can be assessed with regard to its potential transferability (Pearson et al., 2011).

1. Are the characteristics of the original sample of persons, settings, processes (etc.) fully described enough to permit adequate comparisons with other samples?
2. Have limiting effects of sample selection, the setting, history and constructs been discussed?
3. Is the sampling theoretically diverse enough to encourage broader applicability?

The sample of teachers and counselors used in this guide as described in the Sample Section of this report has enough detail to permit adequate comparison to other teachers and counselors. The limited effects of sample setting were discussed in the guide's limitation section. Finally, the sample, which contained teachers and counselors from both sexes and a number of different ethnic groups was diverse enough broader applicability.

Validity in this guide was less threatened by selecting a sample population of teachers and counselors who interact with potential teen Internet sexual assault victims. To determine external validity, data analysis involved counting the frequency of responses to the same question. A greater number of identical responses to questions affecting teen Internet sexual assault such as chat rooms and social networking websites maybe more transferable to the rest of the population than responses that are not identical.

Data Coding

Participant responses were recorded on data collection forms; that data is then transferred to a text database. The database was used as the repository for storing, coding and analyzing collected data. Data were coded when they were transferred from the original collection form (such as a test booklet) into a format that lends itself to data analysis (Marczyk, & et al., 2005).

The interview responses were coded into groups as they were transferred from the written notes and the interviewee voice recordings. Meaning statements were first extracted from significant statements, via process of horizontalization that reflected the participant's opinion on the teen Internet sexual assault experience. During the data coding process duplicate statements or shared experiences between participants were condensed. Crucial elements of the participant's shared opinions were sought out and clustered into themes. Finally, the data coding process added textual descriptions that highlighted the experience, participant quotes added to the richness of the experience.

Data Analysis

Triangulation. According to Leech and Onwuegbuzie (2007) researchers need to utilize at least two, if not more, types of data analysis tools in order to triangulate results. This guide analyzes the Internet teen assault phenomenon from a number of different perspectives; the parent, teen, educators and law enforcement. Triangulation is a means of improving the rigor of the analysis by assessing the integrity of the inferences that one draws from more than one vantage point (Leech & Onwuegbuzie (2007).

Triangulation is not just to pinpoint effects, but is also used as a means to create a common point of view (Shank, 2006). The data was analyzed in this guide from both the male and female participant's perspectives to gain a common point of view of the teen Internet sex phenomenon. This common point of view was forged by looking at how knowledge might be constructed from differing perspectives (Shank, 2006).

Data Analysis. Data analysis used the modified Van Kaam method of phenomenological analysis described by Moustakas (1994) to capture the essence of the participants' experience regarding teen Internet sexual assault. Because the modified Van Kaam method was used in this guide, data analysis software was not be used. Each interview transcript was reviewed using a modified Van Kaam method. This modified Van Kaam method, described by Moustakas (1994), has seven steps to use for each participant interview.

The steps in this modified Van Kaam method are: (1) listing and preliminary grouping; (2) reduction and elimination; (3) clustering and thematizing the invariant constituents; (4) final identification of the invariant constituents and themes by application; (5) constructing an individual textural description of the experience; (6) constructing an individual structural description and (7) constructing a textural-structural description for each participant.

The following steps were used to transcribe each participant's interview:

Step I.	All words that were important to their perception of teen Internet sexual assault phenomena were written down.
Step II.	Two questions were asked while eliminating words; are they necessary for understanding the perception and is it possible to abstract and label them?
Step III.	The main points were grouped into themes.
Step IV.	The interview transcripts were read a

second time to ensure that the perception of the phenomena was clearly expressed, compatible, and relevant.

Step V.   Direct quotes from the participants that added clarity to the themes were noted.

Step VI.   The participant's clarifying descriptions and imaginative variations from the central themes were noted.

Step VII. A picture was framed by organizing the words, themes, descriptions and variations from the interviews. (Moustakas, 1994)

In qualitative research, information is organized and a coherent picture or reflection of intertwined concepts is created by following a process (Neuman, 2003). Through a text analysis, this guide attempted to identify trends in teen introversions and extroversions. The analysis also included the role of anonymity in the teen Internet sexual assault phenomenon.

A text database categorized, organized and segmented interview responses to identify data trends and discrepancies. The repository for the qualitative data in this guide was a text database. The data analysis process of this guide included calculating the average responses as well as the range of responses to questions on Internet teen assault. For example, interviewees were asked if they feel that chat rooms are places where predators meet teens.

Based on the responses, chat rooms can be characterized as places where predators are most likely to meet teens. The data analysis portion of this guide evaluated the range of responses. The range is the difference between the highest and the lowest scores in a distribution (Marczyk, & et al., 2005). The range of the responses to an interview question assisted in the determination of whether the responses potentially played a role in the phenomenon.

This guide was used to identify trends and patterns in teen Internet behavior and the effects of those trends on the teen Internet sexual assault phenomenon. For example, this guide explored trends in chat room behavior as well as behavior on social networking websites.

Data Interpretation

Data interpretation involved identifying similarities among the responses that potentially uncovered trends or central tendencies to assist in defining the phenomenon. Interpreting the interview responses involved examining the data to find information not obvious from the individual interview responses alone. Interviewee responses were organized so that meaning and trends were derived from the collected data. Interpretation tends to consist of stating the larger meaning of the discoveries (Creswell, 2008).

Data Presentation

The research report presents the data in a way that best explains the results. The report follows a logical flow that presents the data in a way that increases its understandability. Research reports tend to use flexible, emerging structure and evaluative criteria (Creswell, 2008).

The research report contains enough flexibility to accurately display the gathered data. Interview responses were evaluated based on objective criteria. This guide presents data collected from the qualitative interviews in a realistic and logical report. The report gives an accurate account of interviewee responses and is organized and presented in a manner that realistically outlines the teen Internet sexual assault phenomenon.

Limiting Research Bias

The interviews, during data analysis, and interpretation remained unbiased and reflexive. Reflexivity means the researcher reflects on his or her own biases, values and assumptions and actively writes them into the research guide (Creswell, 2008). The researcher's role as an advocate of protecting teenager from predators on the Internet and the values of supporting effective teenage Internet use is discussed in this guide.

Researchers could make conscious efforts to remain objective and unbiased throughout the research process. The research questions and responses in this guide were examined for bias and the bias was reduced to the greatest extent possible. This guide did not take a reflexive approach from the researcher's perspective. Bias is addressed by: (a) noting that the researcher has nine teenage nieces and nephews that spend a considerable amount of time surfing the Internet; (b) allowing each participant to share his or her experience uninterrupted, except to clarify a point and (c) creating a comfortable rapport and environment for the interview.

Summary

This chapter outlined the research method and design for the qualitative, guide on teen Internet assault. The appropriateness of using qualitative versus quantitative and mixed research methods was also discussed. The chapter outlined the criteria for selecting the sample population of 25 teachers/counselors who have experience interacting with teenaged Internet sexual assault victims. Those teachers/counselors were asked open-ended questions about their opinion on the causes of teen Internet assault. A discussion on data collection procedures and the use of data collection forms took place in this chapter. The chapter also outlined the text database that was used for data analysis and segmenting. Data interpretation, outlined in the chapter, involved determining meaning from the frequency, range and average responses to the interview questions. The chapter described a logical results presentation in a report that readers will find understandable.

This chapter covered this guide's trade-off between internal and external validity. The guide addressed validity questions about the study's sample; therefore possibly giving the study's results transferability, meaning that it may be possible to transfer the responses of the sample to other teachers and counselors. The chapter also covered the reduction of researcher bias in this guide. Finally, chapter 4 covered this guide's results and findings.

CHAPTER **4**

Results

Introduction

A QUALITATIVE, PHENOMENOLOGICAL study was conducted to explore the causes of 13 to 17 year-old teenagers falling victim to child predators on the Internet and it was designed to obtain knowledge by allowing teachers/counselors to answer open ended interview questions about their opinions on the lived Internet sexual assault experiences of teenagers. Semi-structured interviews were used to explore six research questions, and 25 interviews were conducted to explore this phenomenon. As van Manen (1990) described, these interviews served to explore and gather information to more fully develop understanding of a human phenomenon, and as a means to establish a conversation about their opinions on the phenomenon with the interviewees. Interviews were conducted with teachers and counselors in each of their classrooms located at a Midwestern United

States town High School. The interviews were conducted while classes were not in session.

The data were analyzed using the modified Van Kaam method described by Moustakas (1994) to discover invariant constituents and themes from the participant's verbal data. The modified van Kaam (1984) process is used to describe how individuals perceive, conceptualize, and understand a common experience as demonstrated by Moustakas (1994), who focused on identification of key themes in the perception of like-minded people to determine the meaning around a given set of experiences. The purpose of this study was to explore how teenagers fall victim to Internet sexual predators, permitted respondent's voices to be heard and themes to be identified. High school teachers who deal extensively with teenagers were able to provide their opinion on the teen Internet sexual assault phenomenon, thereby revealing aspects of the phenomenon that are not directly numeric or observed (Creswell, 2002). Chapter 4 contains the information obtained from the pilot study, this study's findings, and themes identified from the examination of the data.

Pilot Study

A pilot study was conducted (a) to ascertain that the research questions were valid, (b) to determine an effective sequence of the questions, (c) to identify needed clarification for each research question and (d) to determine the preferred gratuity card for participants. After the taped interview, pilot study respondents were asked about aptness of the research questions, any needed clarifications and the sequencing of the questions. Five teachers were interviewed for the pilot study; the pilot study datum was not included with the sample study analysis. Pilot study respondents indicated no change was needed with the research questions supporting the tenet that the questions were valid and appropriate.

Research Study Sample

The respondents for this study consisted of 25 High School teachers/counselors in a town in the Midwestern United States. Sixteen or 64% were females and 9 or 36% were male. The teachers had one to five children of their own (see *Figure 3*).

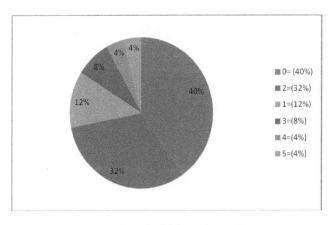

Figure 3. Number of Children of Sample Group

Participant ethnicity was asked to disclose demographic findings of the study sample. The population of this Midwestern United States town is diverse and generally follows the national population. The research study sample reflected the diversity of the State.

The ethnicity of study participants was (a) Caucasian, 73%; (b) Hispanic, 12%; (c) Black, 8%; (d) Pacific Islander, 4%; and (e) Mixed, 4%. One participant indicated a mixed ethnicity—one of Caucasian and Hispanic. No Asian ethnicities were interviewed. Table 1 illustrates the diverse ethnicity of the study sample group as compared to the United States and the State of Arizona's population. *Figure 4* shows just the sample group ethnicity. Sixteen teachers who were contacted chose not to participate in the study, while 20 teachers could not be reached.

Ethnicity	US	Midwestern US State	Study Sample
Caucasian	74.8%	73%	76%
Black	13.6%	4.1%	8%
Hispanic	16.3%	29.6%	8%
Pacific Islander	0.02%	0.02%	4%
Mixed Ethnicity	1.6%	1.6%	4%

Table 1. Ethnicity of Sample Study (United States Census Bureau, 2010)

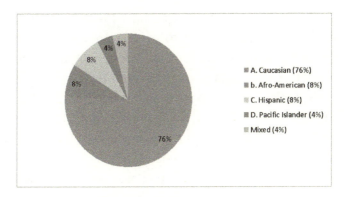

Figure 4. Sample Group Ethnicity

Interview Questions

Analysis of the six interview questions in the 25 interviews was completed by manual review using the modified Van Kaam method. Each respondent's interview was read, re-read and a list of expressions relevant to the participant's experiences were noted (Moustakas, 1994). Key expressions were listed for each respondent.

Horizontalization recognizes participant statements as relevant to the question and of equal value, creating a horizon of limitless possibilities (Moustakas, 1994). The responses of each of the participants had the same weight. From the horizontalization process meaning or meaning units are formed (Moustakas, 1994).

Invariant constituents were then identified, leading to clusters, and from the clusters five themes were identified. Themes established for each interview question were: interview question 1 - circumstances likely to cause a teen to meet a predator on the internet; interview question 2 - tools likely used by teens to meet predators on the Internet, for example MySpace™ and Facebook®; interview question 3 - the role that teen needs play in the likelihood that they will meet a predator on the Internet; interview question 4 - the role that a teen needs to play in the likely hood that they will meet a predator on the Internet; interview question 5 - possible solutions to the phenomenon. The interview transcripts are located in Appendix E that includes a table of contents for easy access to each participant interview.

Interview Question 1. Interview question 1 asked: Please share with me your opinion on what circumstances most likely lead to teenage sexual encounters with someone whom they meet on the Internet? The purpose of the question was twofold - (1) to understand the circumstances that a teen maybe dealing with, and (2) to gain insight about social circumstances which may lead to an encounter with a predator. A further benefit of the question was to establish a conversational tone, or as (Shank, 2002) described a grand tour question that invites the participant to lead in their sharing.

Interview Question 2. Interview question 2 asked: Please share with me your opinion on how teenagers will most likely meet people on the Internet; for example, in a chat room, on Facebook®, on MySpace™

or something totally different? Participant responses cited Facebook® (14/39 or 37%) as the primary way that teens meet predators on the Internet, while (6/39 or 14%) of the participant say that MySpace™ as the primary meeting place between teens and predators.

Interview Question 3. Interview question 3 asked: What role do you feel that a teen's personality; for example, introverted, extroverted or something totally different plays a role in whether they will meet a predator on the Internet?

a. Do you feel that an introverted teen is more likely to attract a predator?
b. Do you feel that an extroverted teen is more likely to attract a predator?

Participant responses cited both introverted and extroverted personalities (6/26 or 26%) as playing a primarily role in whether a teen would meet a predator on the internet, while participants choose an introverted personality (4/26 or 13%) as the second most likely personality trait that would lead to a teen meeting a predator on the Internet.

Interview Question 4. Interview question 4 asked: Please share with me your opinion on the role that teen gratification (for example, sex, companionship, self-esteem or something else plays in whether a teen will meet an Internet predator? Participant responses cited a need for a relationship (12/33 or 36%) as the primary teen need or gratification which would lead to a teen sexual relationship with someone whom they met on the Internet, while low self-esteem was the second most popular response (4/33 or 12%) as to what need or gratification would lead to a teen meeting a predator on the Internet.

Interview Question 5. Interview question 5 asked: Please share with me your opinion on what support would most likely help; for example, more parental supervision, better law enforcement, better High School curriculum or other to prevent your contact with an Internet Predator? Participant responses cited better parental support (19/36 or 53%) as the primary support that would help teens avoid establishing relationships with predators on the Internet, while (5/36 or 14%) say that community education is the best way to prevent teens from meeting predators on the Internet.

Development of Themes

Theme 1 – Lack of Parental Supervision. Participant responses cited lack of parental supervision (12/40 or 30%) as the primary circumstance most likely lead to teenage sexual encounters with someone whom they meet on the Internet. Lack of parental support was the most common circumstance cited by participants (12/40) that lead to teenagers meeting predators on the Internet. Some participants stated that a dysfunctional family, lack of parental supervision and caring can facilitate a teen gravitating to the Internet to meet a potential predator. Participant D stated that, "dysfunctional families and lack of caring environment in the home can lead to teens meeting predators on the Internet" (see Appendix E, p. 132).

Theme 2 – Anonymity. The ability to hide or falsify identity (anonymity) (5/40 or 15%) was commonly a co-occurring issue. The results show that because of anonymity on the Internet, teenagers and predators are able to role-play and hide their identity. Participant Q stated that some teenagers are, "shy in social situations-this keeps them at a distance/ curiosity/anonymity."

Theme 3 – Loneliness. Participant responses cited teen loneliness (6%) Previous studies have shown that teenage Internet sexual behavior is related to loneliness. Participant J mentioned that some teenagers seek relationships on the Internet because of loneliness; "they want to behave as adults, but do not have parental guidance" (see Appendix E, p. 144).

Theme 4 – Additional Circumstances. Some participants provided multiple responses to some of the interview questions. Two participants responses each (6%) stated teen lack of social skills, (6%) teen use of Facebook®, (6%) use of cell phones. One response each (3%) teen peer pressure, (3%) inability for form relationships, (3%) photos on social media, (3%) using Twitter©, (3%) no Internet blocks on home computer, (3%) rebellion against parents, (3%) lack of education about predators, (3%) dysfunctional family, (3%) boredom, (3%) sympathy for predators, (3%) what teens see on television.

Theme 5 – Social Networking Websites and Chat rooms. Nearly half of the participants (37%) reported Facebook® as the tool used by predator to lead teenagers into meetings via the Internet. Participant A mentioned that, "our daughter used Facebook®, Yahoo chat rooms, Teenchat, MSN Messenger, and Xat chat" (see Appendix E, p. 124). Myspace™ was also one of the most common websites cited by participants (14/39) as a means for teenage encounters with Internet predators. Participant O believes that, teenagers meet Internet predators on "MySpace™ and Facebook® - Social networks that anyone has access to" (see Appendix E, p. 154).

The current research study sample reflected the gravity of chat room use as 11%. According to Participant G, teenagers meet predators in "chat rooms; anyone can use them and on Facebook® where you have to accept friendships" (see Appendix E, p. 138). According to participant C, teenagers are likely to meet Internet predators on "Facebook®, Twitter© [or other sites that are] easily accessible or possibly Craig's List. Depicted below in *Figure* 6 are ways or tools that teenagers use to form relationships on the Internet which could lead to sexual assault.

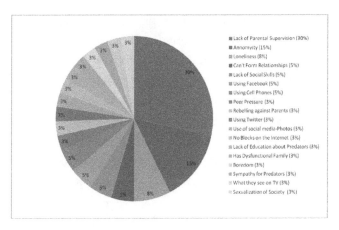

Figure 5. Circumstances Leading to Teen Internet Assault

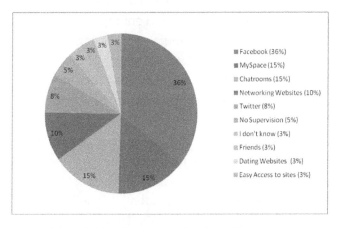

Figure 6. How Teens meet People on the Internet

Theme 6 – Introverted and Extroverted Teen Personality. One fourth of the participants (26%) reported that both introverted and extroverted teenagers were vulnerable to Internet predators. Participant D stated that, "both introverted and extroverted teenagers [are vulnerable to Internet predators] - they will both try to reach out in different ways if they feel a void." The high number of participants said that introverted teenagers were vulnerable was consistent with the literature review. Participant W mentioned that, "they (introverted teens) have not talked with people in the community/they want attention" (see Appendix E, p. 170).

Participant A related that, "we have a daughter who is introverted and she does not seek relationships with boys, whereas our other daughter is very extroverted and has a very high interest in boys" (see Appendix E, p. 124). Nine percent of the participants reported that easily manipulated teenagers could fall prey to Internet predators. Participant A mentioned that, "she [her daughter] has low self-esteem, so these factors made her very easy to manipulate" (see Appendix E, p. 124).

Theme 7 – Teenage Rebellion. Four percent of the respondents cited that teenagers seek Internet relationships on the Internet as rebellion against their parents. Participant B mentioned that, "some introverted teenagers meet predators on the Internet as rebellion against traditional family structure and values" (see Appendix E, p. 128). The role of teenage personality in teenage Internet sexual assault is depicted below in *Figure 7*.

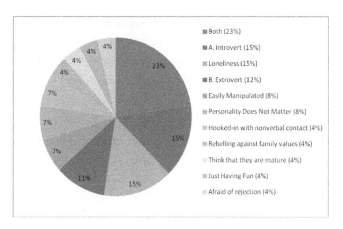

Figure 7. Role of Teenage Personality

Theme 8 – Need for a Relationship. Nearly one-third of the respondents cited a need for relationship as the greatest teenage need leading them to meet someone on the Internet. Participant K mentioned that some teenagers are "looking for relationships online [and are] more susceptible to what others say online" (see Appendix E, p. 146). The participants stated that teens frequent websites seeking relationships. Participant K further explains that "teens go online seeking communication and someone to have a relationship with" (see Appendix E, p. 146).

Theme 9 – Low Self-Esteem. Fourteen percent of the respondents cited teenage low self-esteem as playing a role in teenage encounters with Internet predators. Participant V mentioned that, "self-esteem plays biggest role, and that predators feed on low self-esteem that and keep the teen involved" (see Appendix E, p. 168).

Theme 10 – Instant Gratification. Nearly 12% of the respondents stated that teenagers seek Internet relationship as a form of instant gratification. Participant C stated that teenagers needed "immediate gratification and that they try to have the adult relationship that they see on TV" (see Appendix E, p. 130). *Figure 8* shows the type of teenage need or gratification that motivates teenagers to seek sexual relationships on the Internet.

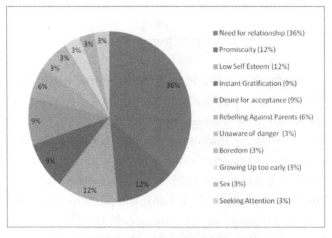

Figure 8. Role of Teenage Need or Gratification

Theme 11– Improved Parental Support. Over half of the respondents cited better parental support as their main source of support needed to prevent teenage Internet sexual assault (19/36 or 53%). Participant K mentioned that, "parental support and connections in school - parents need to know" (see Appendix E,

p. 146). Some of the participants believe that additional parental support and supervision would help reduce the likelihood that a teen will meet an Internet predator. Participant H stated that "additional parental supervision was needed - kids will do what they want on the internet" (see Appendix E, p. 140). One mother attended a parenting class with her toddler, while another participated in a free weekend martial arts program with her daughters.

Theme 12 – Improved Education. A number of the teachers mentioned that education would help prevent teen Internet sexual assault. Participant E mentioned that, "more community education and awareness and parental supervision were needed" (see Appendix E, p. 134).

Theme 13 – Improved Law Enforcement. Some of the participants (9%) said that parental supervision and education were not enough and that law enforcement would have to become more involved to help prevent Internet sexual assault Participant L said that, "law Enforcement [would help] - Parents are always last to know/Kids have hidden lives" (see Appendix E, p. 148). Participants recognized that better connections and relationships in school are an important way to prevent teenage sexual Internet encounters. *Figure 9* displays the type of support that the participants thought would help prevent teenage Internet sexual assault.

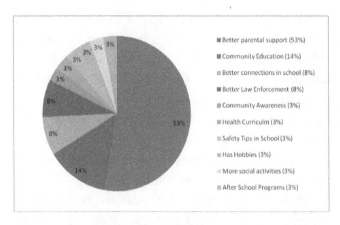

Figure 9. Type of support that could help prevent teenage Internet sexual assault

Figure 10 shows the participants' willingness to answer follow-on questions.

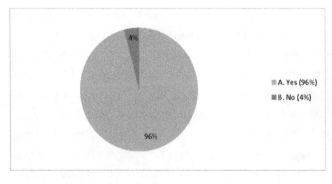

Figure 10. Willingness to answer follow-on questions

Table 2 summarizes the themes and sub-categories within each theme.

Interview Questions	Themes
Circumstances that might lead to encounters with predators	1 Lack of parental support
	2 Anonymity
	3 Loneliness
	4 Additional Circumstances
How teens meet predators	5 Social Networking Websites and Chat rooms
Role Teenage Personality	6 Introverts & Extroverts
	7 Teenage Rebellion
Role Teenage Needs/ Gratification	8 Need for a Relationship
	9 - Instant Gratification
	10 Low Self-esteem
Support for the Teen	11 Improved Parental Support
	12 mproved Education
	13 Improved Law Enforcement

Table 2. Interview Questions and Themes

Summary

The information in chapter 4 presented the results of this qualitative, phenomenological study - through interviews conducted with 25 participants. Five themes were identified: (a) circumstances which most likely lead to teenage Internet sexual assault, (b) how teenagers meet people on the Internet, (c) the role of teenage personality, (d) the role of teenage gratification and (e) what type of support would help. The themes of parental monitoring and support were strong, and consistent with the literature review regarding factors that contributed to teenage Internet sexual assault.

Most notable was the theme that identified the importance of social media websites such as Facebook®, MySpace™ and chat rooms. Even when parental authority was present, participants perceived that teenagers would seek relationships on the Internet as rebellion against that authority. Both introverted and extroverted teenagers could fall prey to predators on the Internet. This finding has implications for educators, parents and mental health professionals that monitor teenage personality and how it affects their Internet activity.

Participants reported that having strong relationships and connections at school would help prevent teenagers from seeking relationships on the Internet. The need for a relationship, loneliness and instant gratification are some of the teenage needs that drive teenagers to predators on the Internet. Participants readily noted positive parental support, healthy relationships and community education, as well as law enforcement, as supportive ways to prevent Internet sexual assault. The conclusions and recommendations of this study are presented in chapter 5.

Conclusions

THE PURPOSE OF this guide is to explore the causes of 13 to 17 year-old teenagers falling victim to child predators on the Internet. Teenagers are a vulnerable population with challenging issues and needs while growing up and using the Internet. Understanding the unique needs of this population, their different experiences and requirements may help create solutions to their falling prey to Internet predators.

Teenagers who experience encounters with Internet predators can have devastating consequences later in life; furthermore, teenagers who use the Internet and could possibly meet predators, represents a growing population of Internet users. According to Chien and Hsinyi (2011), the Taiwan Ministry of Education has recognized the Internet's possible risks and has initiated the island-wide *Teacher Awareness of Internet Safety* (*TAIS*) project for elementary and middle school teachers since 2000. The information

in chapter 5 presents (a) the implications, (b) limitations of this guide, (b) recommendations for future
research, (c) recommendations for practitioners in education, parents, and law enforcement, (d) a summary
of the current research guide and (e) the conclusions.

Implications

Teenagers are a vulnerable population with challenging issues and needs while growing up and using
the Internet. This current guide investigated the circumstances, tools, personality and needs which lead to teenage sexual encounters with Internet predators. Although
the Internet has many positive aspects, one of the most
pernicious aspects is its potential use for online sexual
predation (Dombrowski et al., 2004). A qualitative, phenomenological design was used to hear directly from 25
High School teachers concerning how they chose social
supports.

Notably, respondents stated that parental support
was a major source of support and assistance for teenagers. This finding was interesting because 16% of participants reported community education. Whereas during
the interviews 9% of the respondents reported law enforcement as the main source of support for teenagers in
the prevention of Internet sexual assault. In 2009, among
a Midwestern US State youth in 9th through 12th grades,
14% of girls and 7% of boys reported being physically
forced to have sexual intercourse when they did not want
to (Midwestern US State Department of Education, 2010).

A need for a relationship drives some teenagers to seek companionship on the Internet, often resulting in and predatory relationships. One teacher reported that her daughter was very defiant in the home, but with the predator she was willing to do anything for him to make him happy because she was afraid of rejection. According to Vorauer, Cameron, Holmes and Pearce (2003), four studies demonstrated that fears of rejection prompt individuals to exhibit a signal amplification bias, whereby they perceive that their overtures communicate more romantic interest to potential partners than is actually the case. Participant A: We also suspect that she [their daughter] fears rejection because her biological father signed away his parental rights when she was two, and has had no contact with her.

Interview Questions

The overarching question for this research was *protecting teens that use the Internet*. To investigate this phenomenon six interview questions were asked. Themes were developed following a modified Van Kaam method to build a textural structural description of the teenage Internet sexual assault phenomenon.

Development of Themes

Theme 1 – Lack of Parental Supervision. Participant's shared stories of what they believe are circumstances which lead teenagers to meet sexual predators on the Internet. Lack of parental supervision was the most recognized issue by respondents as 30% cited this as a reason for how teenagers can meet predators on the Internet. The lack of monitoring from parents as to what a child is doing [can give teenagers the opportunity to form relationships on line] (Pilot Participant 1). Teenage Internet users need parental/adult supervision - someone who cares for the child (Participant G).

Over one fourth of the participants (30%) indicated a lack of parental supervision as a major circumstance leading to teenage Internet sexual assault. These assaults can leave both physical and emotional scares. According to Taylor (2006) Ringland, a self-taught Information Technology (IT) expert, even persuaded one of his young victims to meet him, and while on bail for the original webcam offences, was caught in bed with her (One of the youngsters described her ordeal as 'Internet rape' and even spoke of committing suicide. Low self-esteem among teenagers also contributed to their seeking relationships on the internet.

Theme 2 – Anonymity. The teachers/counselors reported that 15% believed that its anonymity is a circumstance that might lead to teens meeting predators on the Internet. According to Kelly, Lord and Marcus (2000), there is something about the impersonal and anonymous nature of the Web that makes it easier to say things and do things you would not do if it was were a face-to-face encounter. Facebook® was mentioned most often as the teenager's first source of contact on the Internet while MySpace™ was cited as second most. These websites were described as providing anonymity, unmonitored access and a growing way for teenagers to develop friendships. Participants reported that Facebook® provided (a) anonymity; (b) lack of adult supervision, (c) easy for teenagers to use and (d) 24-hours a day/seven days a week availability.

Chael (n.d.) stated that child predators have become adept in exploiting their perversion and hiding behind the anonymity of the Internet, making it difficult for law enforcement to identify these predators. Participant L said that, "law Enforcement [would help] - Parents are always last to know/Kids have hidden lives" (see Appendix E, p. 148). According to Elisheva (2004), empirical research on adults has similarly emphasized the opportunities for role experimentation, identity play and online relationship development provided by the unique features of the Internet (e.g., anonymity, absence of geographic and temporal constraints). The results show that because of anonymity on the Internet, teenagers and predators are able to role-play and hide their identity.

Theme 3 – Loneliness. Seeking positive relationships outside of the Internet is also an active process that most teenagers can pursue to prevent loneliness and to develop a sense of belonging. Participant H described "loneliness and a wish to connect, low self-esteem, no parental guidance" as important circumstances leading to teenage Internet sexual assault, (see Appendix E, p.

138). A further point in terms of how teenage personality affects their Internet use, introverted teenagers have insecurities and are looking for acceptance in other places (Participant C, see Appendix E, p. 160).

Öztürk and Özmen (2011) stated that researches proved that a new psychological disorder of problematic Internet use was associated with individual characteristics as loneliness, shyness, anxiety, depression, personality type, and self-cognition. The current research study sample (15%) reflected that loneliness is the third circumstance which might lead to teenagers meeting predators on the Internet. With increasing Internet use, introverts were less involved in local communities and felt lonelier than extroverts (Peter et al., 2005).

Theme 4 – Additional Circumstances. Some participants provided multiple responses to some of the interview questions. Two participants responses each (6%) stated teen lack of social skills, (6%) teen use of Facebook®, (6%) use of cell phones. One response each (3%) teen peer pressure, (3%) inability for form relationships, (3%) photos on social media, (3%) using Twitter©, (3%) no Internet blocks on home computer, (3%) rebellion against parents, (3%) lack of education about predators, (3%) dysfunctional family, (3%) boredom, (3%) sympathy for predators, (3%) what teens see on television.

Theme 5 – Use of Social Networking Websites and Chat rooms. The prevalent use of Facebook®,

MySpace™ and chat rooms for contact with predators was consistent with prior research, and a significant highlight in this guide. Participants perceived these social websites as an important part of teenager social contact even when the relationship may lead to contact with predators. Facebook® was mentioned most often as the teenager's first source of contact on the Internet while MySpace™ was cited as second most. These websites were described as providing anonymity, unmonitored access and a growing way for teenagers to develop friendships.

Eleven percent recognized networking websites in general as Internet tools which led to teenage encounters with Internet predators. Another highlight from this guide is the affect of dating websites and Twitter© as tools. Thirty-seven percent of participants reported Facebook® as a source for teenagers to meet people and subsequently predators on the Internet; this source was further described as being open to the public and very easy for teenagers to use. Participants reported that Facebook® provided (a) anonymity; (b) lack of adult supervision, (c) easy for teenagers to use and (d) 24-hours a day/seven days a week availability.

Nearly all respondents reported that social websites such as Facebook®, MySpace™ and Twitter© led to regular teenage social contact on the Internet and expressed the belief that greater parental supervision would help solve the issue even though parental Internet knowledge may be limited. Participant D described social websites as, "easily open and accessible to students - particularly newer sites" (see Appendix E, p. 129).

Theme 6 – Introverted and Extroverted Teen Personalities. Many respondents indicated that talking to others, whether formally or informally would help prevent both introverted and extroverted teenagers from seeking relationships on the Internet. Findings from interview question 3 led to a theme of how a teenager's personality affects their use of the Internet. Aspects of this theme included: (a) extroversive, (b) introversive, (c) loneliness and (d) manipulation. Huang, Zhang, Li, Wang, Zhang and Tao (2010) stated that certain personality traits such as shyness, introversion and social withdrawal are closely associated with certain types of Internet Addiction Disorder (IAD).

Over 25% of participants stated that both introverted and extraverted teenagers are vulnerable to Internet predators. Under these circumstances, parents and teachers could have a firm understanding of how a teenager's personality affects their use of the Internet. Having supportive parents and healthy relationships outside of the Internet, most respondents expressed as a benefit to teenagers, even though teenagers may not have sought this support from their parents.

Theme 7 – Teenage Rebellion. Rebellion against parents was stated by 3% of the participants as the circumstance most likely leading to teenage sexual encounters with someone whom they meet on the Internet. This was consistent with the literature found in the study by Kelly et al., (2000). A participant in the Kelly et al., (2000) study stated that all along, his parents urged him to go outside, to spend more time with family and peers, but Adam's teen rebellion was to keep logging on. The sense that teenagers are rebellious was the participants' perspective and one on which Michael (n.d.) stated that we all have heard the term "teenage rebellion." Its conventional wisdom that teens go through a period of turbulent adolescence before - it is hoped - they settle down and become mature, productive adults.

While teenage rebellion is nothing new, the Internet can be a breeding ground for bad behavior (Kelly et al, 2000). Participants reported stated a sense that education was an important source of support for easily manipulated teenagers. According to Participant T, education makes them understand they do not know who they are talking to (see Appendix E, p. 162).

Theme 8 – Need for a Relationship. Respondents shared teenaged needs/gratification traits that led to teenage Internet sexual assaults. Their comments ranged from (a) need for a relationship, (b) need for instant gratification and (c) low teenage self-esteem. Participant A stated that "we have a daughter who is introverted and she does not seek relationships with

116

boys, whereas our other daughter is very extroverted and has a very high interest in boys" (see Appendix E, p. 122).

Teen emotional needs were to be listened to, not to be judged, and for others not to assume what their needs were. Instrumental needs such as attention, social contact and acceptance were described as important in the lives of teenagers. Participant W stated that "teenage needs vary, extroverted teenagers need outside attention, but introverted teenagers need social contact and acceptance" (see Appendix E, p. 168).

Theme 9 – Instant Gratification. Instant gratification and desire for acceptance issues was complex and intertwined in the difficulties leading to teenage encounters with Internet predators. These two issues hindered how much support a parent could truly provide to teenagers. Formal support that combined parenting, education and law enforcement required follow through, and appeared to give teenagers the best opportunity to develop abilities to avoid predators on the Internet.

Because these needs frequently overlapped into varied areas, an integrated approach between parents, education, and criminal justice could be formed. Participant C stated that stated that "[teens want] immediate gratification - having the adult relationship that they see on TV (see Appendix E, p. 168).

Theme 10 – Low Self-Esteem. The attention that a teenager receives on the Internet plays a role in determining their self-identity and self-esteem. According to Kaili and Tan (2010), four main spiritual needs were reported by adolescent girls: body image, a sense of self, relationships and future. Teenage emotional changes can initiate a need for emotional support that supports dialogue between parent and teenager.

The emotional and psychological needs of adolescents in their body image, a sense of self, relationships and their future reflect an underlying personal quest to achieve a stable positive self-identity (Kaili & Tan, 2010). A teenager, stressed with chronic worry about self-identity, self-esteem, relationships and acceptance is able to avoid fulfilling these needs on the Internet through parental support and education.

Theme 11 – Improved Parental Support. The prevalence of parental supports for teenagers may reflect a reassurance because parents are a known entity while educational supports require one to be open to school rules and contact with teachers and counselors (Valcke et al., 2010). Two dimensions are distinguished in Internet parenting styles: parental control and parental warmth. Meanwhile, parents who are "always there" offered a consistent source of emotional as well as instrumental assistance such as watching their children when they surf the Internet.

Participant F stated the importance of "parental support and connections in school - Parents need to know" (see Appendix E, p. 134). Parents sometimes find it difficult to convince easily manipulated teenagers that they are being manipulated and to leave those manipulative relationships. But even with more legal and media attention, the challenge for parents and other authorities remains the same - helping the girl to see her situation clearly so she actually wants to leave (Dominus, 2004).

Overall, participants stated that teenagers were not likely to ask parents or friends for support, although formal supports such as school staff, social services, or mental health counselors are readily accepted supports, as well as family. A strong notion for many participants was the need to advocate for parental supervision, described by Pilot 3: "more parental supervision and more parent involvement would help" (see Appendix F, p. 187).

Easily manipulated teenagers and teenagers who think that they are mature were sub-themes in the role that teenage personality plays.

Parental contact was important for the participants to help teenagers recognize when they are being manipulated. Dominus (2004) explains that for teenage abusers, manipulation often precedes violence. Sometimes it starts with a cell phone as a gift that turns into a girlfriend-homing device, which becomes a means of tracking her every move. Participant S shared that, "he [predator] did a great job of manipulating her feelings and weaknesses. He really got to know her and took on a parental role when it fit or was very loving towards her as a boyfriend" (see Appendix E, p. 160).

Theme 12 – Improved Education. A number of the teachers mentioned that education would help prevent teen Internet sexual assault. Participant E mentioned that, "more community education and awareness and parental supervision were needed" (see Appendix E, p. 134). According to Dombrowski, LeMasney, Ahia and Dickson (2004), when attempting to protect children from online solicitation, one could include not only technological but also psycho-educational measures of protection. Better education could potentially help protect teenagers from Internet predators. Participant T states that education can "make them [teenagers] understand they do not know who they are talking to" (see Appendix E, p. 134).

Theme 13 – Improved Law Enforcement. Support for better law enforcement or teenage peer support received less immediate recognition as ways to prevent teen Internet assault in the participants' reporting, but were recognized as means to prevent Internet predator contact. Participants acknowledged community awareness and school safety tips as helpful for teenagers. Other formal support resources identified by participants were after school programs and social activities. All participants believed that teenagers could receive some level of support from parents and their local High School.

Limitations of Guide

Limitations in the current guide are related to (a) the study design, (b) researcher bias, (c) small geographic area and (d) the use of personal interviews. In a phenomenological study, interaction and interpretation guide the process with participants and data gathering (Burns & Grove, 2001). Interview data cannot be replicated, as would occur with a quantitative research method.

A small sample size, another hallmark of qualitative studies, limits the ability to generalize study findings; also, the purposive sample limits data gathering to only participants who have experienced the phenomenon under study (Burns & Grove, 2001). This sample is limited to teachers/counselors who have actual experience with counseling teen Internet sexual assault victims. Subjectivity is a potential limitation in a qualitative, phenomenological study and requires acknowledgment of potential biases (Neuman, 2003).

Identified potential biases include the investigator has watched a number of documentaries on the teenage Internet sexual assault phenomenon. To mitigate potential biases, interviews followed the interview questions and focused steadfastly on the participants telling and responses to their experiences that were then transcribed in their entirety to maintain auditability of the investigation. Personal interviews also add limitations as participant responses are considered to be truthful accounts as reported (Shank, 2002).

Furthermore, because of the personal nature of the interview, participants often shared experiences beyond those being investigated. During the pilot study, the interviewer recognized the conversational tone of the semi-structured interview allowed participants to share other personal stories. To maintain the interview focus, the interview questions were shared with the participant before and during the interview.

When a participant expressed tangential data, their comments were acknowledged in a neutral manner or reframed to determine clarity and understanding. Using a conversational approach allowed the participant to openly express his or her thoughts, and may have provided insight to the interviewee as well as to the interviewer (K'Vale, 1996; Shank, 2002).

Recommendations for Future Research

Recommendations for future research would improve the guide design by overcoming noted study limitations such as: (a) changing the wording of the interview questions, (b) using a purposive sample of actual teenagers and (c) identifying specific parents involved with teenaged victims. In future research, wording questions in a more personal manner would be recommended such as to tell the researcher about the circumstances which lead to a teen meeting a predator on the Internet. Also interview question 5 – such ask what support would have prevented you from meeting a predator (if the actual teens were interviewed), and interview question 6 - what was least helpful to you.

The purposive sample of teachers for this guide worked with teenagers in local high schools. Teachers from special education schools were not included in the research sample because the literature review cited less Internet use among special education teenagers. As the research study progressed, a distinction was found in the type of support that respondents recommended for teenagers depending on whether they had children of their own.

Teachers without children recommended more increased parental support than those that did not have children. Future studies would benefit by narrowing the purposive sample to only those teachers with teenagers of their own or those without teenagers. This comparative study would compare the responses of teachers with teenagers with the responses with those without teenagers. Also, participants with children recommended a greater mix of formal and informal support for teenagers. Forty-seven percent of the respondents reported that some type of parental support was needed to prevent teenagers from falling victim to Internet predators.

Having parental support possibly affected the teenager's concept of feeling accepted. Future studies would benefit by identifying support resources early in the interview. A further suggestion for investigation would be to add teenage peers as a support source.

Wurtele and Kenny (2010) shared the view that protection of children and efforts to decrease the prevalence of these [Internet] potential sexual offenses could come in the form of education.

New areas of research recommended from the findings of this guide would continue to elucidate measures that support safe teenage use of the Internet. Research in the disciplines of parenting, education and law enforcement would benefit by investigating their unique services and interactions with teenagers to determine outcomes resulting from their interventions; particularly beneficial would be a longitudinal study of outcomes. A longitudinal study of teenage Internet sexual assault victims would provide data about their progression in (a) the use of specific supports, (b) changes initiated by the support such as new educational programs and (c) changes initiated by the participant such as mentoring, interventions and counseling for teenagers.

Another area for researchers could be investigating interdisciplinary collaboration to help prevent Internet assaults on teenagers. Areas to investigate might involve parenting, education and law enforcement or a combination of two or more disciplines working cooperatively with teenagers. Research about integration of services may enhance collaboration between service providers and teenagers, eliminate costly duplication of services, as well as lessen competition for funding (Welch, 2007).

Other researchers may wish to use a quantitative study to investigate if there is a correlation between the number of parents in the household and its effect on teenage Internet behavior. A study of this nature may use both single parent and dual parent households as the study sample. Further inquiry may lead to a quantitative, explanatory study to investigate what effect a relationship with older teenagers or siblings has on younger teenagers, investigating how that support affects their Internet choices, and general sense of well-being.

A causal model may also be promising to disclose the causal relationship. Correlation cannot disclose the causal relationship. Research into the family situation when supporting teenager use of the Internet may increase knowledge about the dynamics of a family during this challenging period. Teenage peer or sibling relationships from a gender perspective of female and male during a period when teenagers are heavily involved with the Internet may guide researchers toward knowledge about identity changes, identity conflict, as well as the benefit of having or not having teenage peer or sibling relationships during this period. Participant A stated, "I think adolescents respond well to peer groups" (see Appendix E, p. 122).

Implications and Recommendations for Practitioners

Educators, policy makers and leaders in the disciplines of parenting, education and law enforcement may use the following implications and recommendations. Findings from this study may provide new information for those who work with teenagers. Furthermore, new ideas in providing support and services to teenagers may be generated.

Recommendations for Parents. The parents and grandparents in the lives of teenagers provide a critical level of support, both emotional and instrumental. Participant Y believes that "parental supervision [is needed but] parents get busy and teachers can only do so much" (see Appendix E, p. 172). Parents could be concerned about the growing increase of teenaged Internet use. Despite the many benefits, the explosive growth in the popularity of these [social networking] sites has generated concerns among parents about the potential risks of posting personal information and contact with strangers, some of whom may be sexual predators (Wurtele & Kenny, 2010).

Increasing parental support and control of teenage Internet use was acknowledged by participants as beneficial to the prevention of teenage Internet sexual assault. Parents, by watching television documentaries or by reading local and regional publications may pass information along to their teenage children. The media has fueled parental anxiety by warning parents about cyber predators who sift through online profiles and social networking sites to identify potential targets (Wurtele & Kenny, 2010).

Parents can direct regular updates and distribution

of Internet predator information to their teenagers. Only 25% of youths who received an online sexual solicitation informed a parent (Wurtele & Kenny, 2010). Another component parents may develop is a network of communication with other parents to encourage caring and role-modeling for their teenagers.

Recommendations for Educators and Mental Health Care Professionals. Generally, education for teenagers focuses on academics and does not place a priority on the emotional concerns of teenagers. Public education, unfortunately, tends to place great emphasis on academic achievements and ignore the multiple dimensions of human beings; as a result, it often fails to help students maximize their inner, human potentials (Kaili & Tan, 2010). Implications from this guide that would support local education agencies are (a) to train staff about the proper use of the Internet, (b) to provide support and outreach to teen-aged Internet sexual assault victims that is consistent, easy to find and empathic and (c) to individually tailor services and supports to these teenagers.

Findings in this guide suggest education personnel and mental health professionals have a key opportunity to recognize and develop supportive relationships with teenagers to prevent them from falling victim to Internet predators. Educating parents as well is required, as they did not grow up with ubiquitous digital technology. Educational service staff may be encouraged to have training about needs of teenaged

Internet users as well as how best to interact in a helping manner.

Recommendations for Law Enforcement. Law enforcement is aware of the increasing teenage Internet assault victim population, particularly those on social media websites and in chat rooms. Current information is necessary to guide effective approaches in assisting vulnerable teenage victims. Participant L explains that "law enforcement and parents are always last to know/ Kids have hidden lives" (see Appendix E, p. 146). This guide adds to that information because the findings illustrate the importance of law enforcement support, particularly predator hotlines, as a first line of contact for information and assistance to these teenagers.

Teenage Internet sexual assault deserves attention because of the impact on the emotional development of teenagers and the affects that will have later on in their lives. Law enforcement leaders may use this knowledge to advocate for a wide dissemination of information to the community that surrounds teenaged Internet users. According to Soster and Drenten (2010) most states have legislation requiring schools to include punishment for electronic harassment in safety policies (e.g., suspension/expulsion) as well as electronic stalking/harassment laws, with punishments including fines and imprisonment.

Law enforcement leaders would also want to endorse accessible programs that focus on the primary issues contributing to teenage Internet sexual assault.

Law enforcement leaders may create coalitions by fostering communication. Welch (2007) asserted that communication is key and urged community leaders to remain open-minded and listen to other stakeholders when creating a common purpose and value. Respondents in the current guide shared their distress such as not having enough law enforcement focus on the issue of teenage Internet sexual assault.

Law enforcement leaders have a responsibility to ensure equitable, respectful and confidential services are given to teenaged victims. The findings may be used by law enforcement leaders to provide information and guide training for their staff in sensitizing them to issues of teenage Internet sexual assault. Included in the training would be characteristics that promote listening and trust, and the importance of recognizing and working with informal support systems, mainly family and educators.

Finally, they [predators] deserve the most severe penalty on the book. Natalie (n.d.) stated that the problem will always exist, but with the proper education for parents and children and continuing improvements by law enforcement, we are going to see it tackled. Representative Robert, (n.d.) stated that based on fears about possible victimization of young people by Internet predators, Facebook® has agreed to install a panic button on user pages hosted on its U.K. website so suspicious behavior can be reported to the authorities immediately.

Recommendations for Policy Makers. Recognition of how vulnerable teenagers are on the Internet suggests to policy makers the need to widely disseminate information about how teenagers use the Internet. Alarmingly, teens rarely inform their parents when they receive sexual solicitations online (Wurtele & Kenny, 2010). Policy makers, as with educators, may address personal, emotional and instrumental means to assist teenagers. Policy makers may use findings from this research to address specific services to teenaged Internet users. Participant X stated that "teenagers need less access to computer and more access to sports and open gyms" (see Appendix E, p. 170).

Reflections: An Investigative Journey. Researchers obviously gain personally from taking an investigative journey. The opportunity to pursue a passion in protecting teens, and helping parents is the reward at this journey's end. At this closing, investigators, themselves usually also practitioners and leaders, are ushered into an advanced world of the informed.

Such personal gains, despite their significance as milestones in personal growth, would ring hollow except for the beneficent purposes of advanced studies to add to global knowledge and contribute to society. This researcher hopes this research effort has fulfilled these purposes within its inherent and practical limits. This investigative journey was joined after more than three decades of practice in computing and Internet development; these were the same groundings in practice that required this researcher to take care not to introduce bias into this study. Clearly, the time was at hand to turn to scholarship for some refreshment and further growth of a more diverse nature.

As an investigative learner, this researcher benefitted and grew from the support of a caring and prepared faculty and productive interactions with fellow scholars, none who had taken quite the same journeys in leadership and whose ideas were therefore all the more valuable. In the Management and Organizational Leadership doctoral track, facilitators and authors offered the transformational leadership and organizational development ideas that put into words phenomena learners had seen before but grappled to describe. As the shadows started to grow long in this investigation, it was time to claim the favorite privilege of the doctoral learner—the opportunity to pursue a passion as a means to contribute to knowledge.

As this researcher repeatedly encountered empathy from teachers/counselors, and reflected on authors' insistence of the importance of respect as expressed in their literature, the value of one's own empathy became apparent. Research conducted for this guide on the teen Internet sexual assault phenomenon revealed that teachers/counselors knew of empathy from their lived experiences. Perhaps we could believe that all Internet users learn over time to respect and have empathy for others.

The implication of teenage Internet assault prevention was that the ideas offered or implied by Preston (2007) that rather than give up in despair or pretend that any teen with a decent public education cannot bypass a filter, it is time to step back from failed patterns of government regulation and consider how Internet architecture can be harnessed to create a positive environment. In this researcher's final chapter, while data collection was being undertaken on at a High school in a Midwestern United States town, a reflection formulated: if they can do it—should not advanced scholars/leaders/practitioners renew their efforts to reach out with empathy? So concludes this doctoral journey—at a new chapter.

Review

The purpose of this guide was to explore the causes of 13 to 17 year-old teenagers falling victim to child predators on the Internet. The pilot study resulted in changing the sequence of the interview questions to enhance dialogue with the participant. The change entailed reducing the demographic questions to protect the respondents' privacy, followed by a grand tour question about the participants' views of circumstances leading to teenage Internet sexual assault, then interview questions 2, 3, 4 and 5 about tools, personality, needs and support.

Repeating the meaning of support with the participant was found to be helpful before and as needed during the interview as well as sharing a written copy of the interview questions for the participant to follow throughout the interview. These changes improved the flow and helped focus the interview. A total of 25 interviews were conducted after a pilot study with five high school teachers.

This purposive sample was ethnically diverse for the area, with Caucasians, African Americans, Hispanics and one Pacific Islander. Five themes were identified using a modified Van Kaam method. Themes identified were: (a) circumstances leading to teenage Internet sexual assault, (b) tools used, (c) role of teenage personality, (d) role of teenage needs and (e) prevention support.

Sub-categories within each theme were further categorized from the participants' data. The themes and sub-categories provided the basis for the conclusions and recommendations from this research. According to Pearse (2009), launch of the Government's Click Safe Click Clever initiative, from the UK Council on Child Internet Safety, is the result of a review initiated by Gordon Brown two years ago in which he said he was "not interested in censorship but we do need rules governing aspects of the internet where children are involved."

The varying layers of support; parents, schools and law enforcement provide context to the teenager and their families as to how teenagers see themselves in relation to the resources available. The personal support system includes the parent, schools and law enforcement that affect teenager's daily lives. The strategic support system is more removed from the teenager's everyday life although policy makers influence the teenager through what support is available and the length of the support.

Lastly, the strategic support system, an overarching of the cultural mores of the community, influences how the teenager is perceived and the value of his or her needs. Based on the results of this phenomenological research, teenagers receive support from curriculum and friends at school most often from information shared by their informal peer groups. Participants were more likely to have a wider range of social supports if they were in extracurricular activities such as the band or sports.

Berson and Berson (2003) stated that in school settings; the need to regulate behaviors in cyberspace and minimize potential and actual risks to children has necessitated some governance over harmful interactions. Participants stated that support was important for instrumental assistance, teen emotional support and for their personal needs. Support was improved when the participant reported that teenagers were listened to, had trust and knew the support was dependable. Overall, participants reported most of the support that teenagers needed at home came from parents, while most of the support from school came from teachers and counselors.

Conclusion

Chapter 5 included the implications, limitations, recommendations, summary and conclusions from the study, *How to protect children from Internet predators*. This phenomenological investigation found that parental supervision, education and law enforcement support as the main source of support for teens to help them avoid meeting predators on the Internet. The safety and well-being of children are of paramount importance to schools, and educators have an important role to play in addressing the lapse of preventative intervention (Berson & Berson, 2003).

This finding is important because of the ramifications for parents, educators and law enforcement when planning and implementing support for teenagers. Two recommended measures were more parental supervision and more positive extracurricular activity to keep teenagers occupied. Another significant finding for this sample was the need for a health curriculum, hobbies and social activities.

Teenagers, most likely, use those activities at school through educational supports such as teachers, counselors and friends. Through their parents, teenagers can receive emotional, personal and at times instrumental help to prevent them from seeking relationships on the Internet. Counseling for teenaged Internet sexual assault victims was not a significant finding.

A lack of counseling raises questions about the

availability of such counseling in schools while such services are also affected by cultural values. A subtle finding from this guide, not found in the literature, was that some teens may suffer from hyper activity disorders which make it difficult for them to form normal relationships leading them to relationships online. Further research may explore how parental supervision of teenage Internet use will deter a teenager from engaging with an Internet predator.

It is imperative for schools to recognize the scope of the problem of Internet sexual assault because teenage healthy Internet use is critical for the health of the community at large. Children typically are naïve regarding dangers in cyberspace, and parents often lack familiarity with mechanisms to address these concerns (Berson & Berson, 2003). The results of the current guide are similar to these previous studies, and parents can use the results to advocate for the development of effective support for teenage Internet users to increase their ability to recognize Internet predators, thereby lessening risk of falling victim to them.

References

(2008). Child-porn ring nabbed; Internet fuels abuse, say federal officials. *Contemporary Sexuality, 36*(4), 8. Retrieved from Academic Search Complete database

(2008). Internet law – Communications decency act – Texas district court extends § 230 immunity to social networking sites -- Doe v. MySpace™, Inc., 474 F. Supp. 2d 843 (W.D. Tex. 2007). *Harvard Law Review, 121*(3), 930-937. Retrieved from Business Source Complete database

(2008). Protecting children and teens from cyber-harm. Certain patterns of behavior confer risk; here's what the research shows. *The Harvard Mental Health Letter / From Harvard Medical School, 25*(1), 4-5. Retrieved from MEDLINE with Full Text database

Akers, A., Muhammad, M., & Corbie-Smith, G. (2010). "When you got nothing to do, you do somebody": A community's perceptions of neighborhood effects on adolescent sexual behaviors. *Social Science & Medicine, 72,* 91-99. doi:10.1016/j.socscimed.2010.09.035

Anonymous, (2005). Internet predator jailed for grooming 2 victims; 10 years for chatroom fiend. *Evening Times* (Glasgow)

Anonymous, (2011). FBI seeking email, Facebook access in Phylicia Barnes case, *The Capital*, A.4

Arizona Department of Education (2010). *2009 Arizona youth risk behavior survey trend report*

Ashley, J. (2008). *Child sex exploitation study probes extent of victimization in Illinois,* Research Bulletin, Vol. 6, No. 2, Illinois Criminal Justice Information Authority

Bagwell, K. (2009). Study finds increase in arrests of online child predators. *Education Daily, 42*(97), 3

Bates, A., & Metcalf, C. (2007). A psychometric comparison of internet and non-internet sex offenders from a community treatment sample. *Journal of Sexual Aggression, 13*(1), 11-20. doi:10.1080/13552600701365654

Benner, P. (1994*). Interpretive phenomenology: Embodiment caring, and ethics in health and illness*. Sage Publications Inc.

Berson, M. J., & Berson, I. R. (2003). Lessons learned about schools and their responsibility to foster safety online. *Journal of School Violence, 2*(1), 105-17

Bower, B. (2008). Internet seduction, *Science News,* Washington: Vol. 173, Issue 8.

Burgess, A., Mahoney, M., Visk, J., & Morgenbesser, L. (2008). Cyber child sexual exploitation. *Journal of Psychosocial Nursing & Mental Health Services, 46*(9), 38-45. Retrieved from CINAHL Plus with Full Text database

Burns, N. & Grove, S. (2001). *The practice of nursing research: Conduct, critique and utilization (4th ed)*. W.B. Saunders: Philadelphia, Pennsylvania, USA

Byron, A. (n.d.). Sex predators stalk social media. *USA Today*

Chael, J. (n.d.). Child Internet pornography protection, *FDCH Congressional Testimony*

Chien, C., & Hsinyi, P. (2011). Promoting awareness of Internet safety in Taiwan in-service teacher education: A ten-year experience. *The Internet and Higher Education, 14*(Special Issue; The Internet and Teacher Education: An Asian Experience), 44-53. doi:10.1016/j.iheduc.2010.03.006

Cho, J., & Trent, A. (2006). Validity in qualitative research revisited. *Qualitative Research,6,*319-340.doi:10.1177/1468794106065006

Choo, K. (2009). Responding to online child sexual grooming: An industry perspective. *Trends & Issues in Crime & Criminal Justice,* (379), 1-6. Retrieved from SocINDEX with Full Text database

Cordner, S. (2012, April). *Child porn crackdown heads to House floor.* Retrieved from http://news.wsfu.org

Creswell, J. (2008). *Educational research: Planning, conducting, and evaluating quantitative and qualitative research* (2nd ed.). Upper Saddle River, NJ: Merrill Prentice-Hall

Creswell, J. (2002). *Educational research: Planning, conducting, and evaluating quantitative and qualitative research.* Upper Saddle River, NJ: Merrill, Prentice Hall

Critchlow, K. A. (2005). *A phenomenological study of the career accession of African American females into community college presidencies.* Dissertation, UMI#3202464. Retrieved from ebscohost

DeFranco, J. F. (2011). Teaching Internet security, safety in our classrooms. *Techniques: Connecting Education & Careers, 86*(5), 52

Desjarlais, M., & Willoughby, T. (2010). A longitudinal study of the relation between adolescent boys and girls' computer use with friends and friendship quality: Support for the social compensation or the rich-get-richer hypothesis? *Computers in Human Behavior, 26*(5), 896-905, ISSN 0747-5632, 10.1016/j.chb.2010.02.004

Rimington, D., & Gast, J. (2007). Cybersex use and abuse: Implications for health education. *American Journal of Health Education, 38*(1), 34-40. Retrieved from ProQuest Nursing & Allied Health Source. (Document ID: 1207770421)

Dombrowski, S. C., LeMasney, J. W., Ahia, C., & Dickson, S. A. (2004). Protecting children from online sexual predators: Technological, psychoeducational, and legal considerations. *Professional Psychology: Research And Practice, 35*(1), 65-73. doi:10.1037/0735-7028.35.1.65

Dombrowski, S., Gischlar, K., & Durst, T. (2007). Safeguarding young people from cyber pornography and cyber sexual predation: A major dilemma of the internet. *Child Abuse Review, 16*(3), 153-170. Retrieved from Academic Search Complete database

Dominus, S. (2004). How much do you know about your daughter's boyfriend? *Good Housekeeping, 238*(4), 148

Dylan, W., & Fuller, B. (2010, August). Facebook 'failed to act' on child pornography group, *Illawarra Mercury*, p. 3

Elisheva F. G. (2004). Adolescent internet use: What we expect, what teens report. *Journal of Applied Developmental Psychology, 25*(6), 633-649. doi:10.1016/j.appdev.2004.09.005

Fusilier, M. (2008). An investigation of the integrated model of user technology acceptance: Internet user samples in four countries. *Journal of Educational Computing Research, 38*(2), 155-182

Gallagher, B. (2008). Dangerous worlds? The problems of international and internet child sexual abuse. *Community Safety Journal, 7*(2), 8-11. Retrieved December 17 2009, from Career and Technical Education, (Document ID: 1501067591)

Gallagher, B. (2005). New technology: helping or harming children? *Child Abuse Review, 14*(6), 367-373. doi:10.1002/car.923

Gangadharbatla, H. (2008). Facebook® me: Collective self-esteem, need to belong, and internet self-efficacy as predictors of the iGeneration's attitudes toward social networking sites. *Journal of Interactive Advertising, 8*(2), 1-28

Gilgun, J. F. (2005). Qualitative research and family psychology. *Journal of Family Psychology, 19*(1), 40-50, Retrieved from EBSCOhost

Grant, I. C. (2005), Young peoples' relationships with online marketing practices: An intrusion too far? *Journal of Marketing Management, 21*(5/6), 607-623

Greenfield, P., & Zheng, Y. (2006). Children, adolescents, and the Internet: A new field of inquiry in developmental psychology. *Developmental Psychology, 42*(3). 391-394. doi:10.1037/0012-1649.42.3.391

Hansen, C. (2012, April). *'To Catch a Predator' III*. Retrieved from http:// msnbc.msn.com

Hines, D., & Finkelhor, D. (2007). Statutory sex crime relationships between juveniles and adults: A review of social scientific research. *Aggression & Violent Behavior, 12*(3). 300-314. doi:10.1016/j.avb.2006.10.001

Huang, X., Zhang, H., Li, M., Wang, J., Zhang, Y., & Tao, R. (2010). Mental health, personality, and parental rearing styles of adolescents with Internet addiction disorder. *Cyberpsychology, Behavior and Social Networking, 13*(4), 401-406

Huck, S. W., Beavers, A. S., & Esquivel, S. (2010). Sample. In N. J. Salkind (Ed.). *Encyclopedia of Research Design*. (pp. 1294-1300). Thousand Oaks, CA: SAGE. Retrieved from http://sage-ereference.com/view/researchdesign/n395.xml

Kennison, P. (2005). Child sexual abuse and the internet: Tackling the new frontier. *International Journal of Police Science & Management*; *7*(1), 67-70, 4p

Kelly, K., Lord, M., & Marcus, D. (2000, September). False promise. *U.S. News & World Report*, *129*(12), 48, 7p, 6

Johnson, W., McGue, M., & Iacono, W. G. (2009). School performance and genetic and environmental variance in antisocial behavior at the transition from adolescence to adulthood. *Developmental Psychology*, *45*(4). 973-987. doi:10.1037/a0016225

Kaelin, L. (2012, April). *Report: child abuse hidden in legitimate looking sites*. Retrieved from http://www.techspot.com

Kaili Chen, Z., & Tan, C. (2010). Exploring the Spiritual Needs of Adolescent Girls, *Religion & Education*, *37*(2). 146-161. doi:10.1080/15507394.2010.486369

Lee, S. (2009). Online communication and adolescent social ties: Who benefits more from Internet use? *Journal of Computer-Mediated Communication*, *14*(3). 509-531. doi:10.1111/j.1083-6101.2009.01451.x

Levine, K. L. (2006). The intimacy discount: prosecutorial discretion, privacy, and equality in the statutory rape caseload. *Emory Law Journal*, *55*(4). 691-749

Loughlin, J., & Taylor-Butts, A. (2009). Child luring through the Internet. Juristat: Canadian Centre for Justice Statistics, 29(1). 1B, 4B, 5B, 6B, 7B, 8B, 9B, 10B, 11B, 12B, 13B, 14B, 15B, 16B, 17B. Retrieved from CBCA Complete. (Document ID: 1887488021)

Malesky, L. (2007). Predatory online behavior: Modus operandi of convicted sex offenders in identifying potential victims and contacting minors over the Internet. *Journal of Child Sexual Abuse*, *16*(2). 23-32. Retrieved from Academic Search Complete database

Marczyk, G., DeMatteo, D., & Festinger, D. (2005). *Essentials of research design and methodology.* John Wiley & Sons

McCarthy, J. A. (2010). Internet sexual activity: A comparison between contact and non-contact child pornography offenders. *Journal of Sexual Aggression, 16*(2). 181-195. doi:10.1080/13552601003760006

Michael, S. (n.d). Let's smarten up on teen rebellion. *The Washington Times*

Mishna, F., McLuckie, A., & Saini, M. (2009). Real-world dangers in an online reality: A qualitative study examining online relationships and cyber abuse. *Social Work Research, 33*(2). 107-118. Retrieved from Academic Search Complete database

Nair, A. (2006). Mobile phones and the Internet: Legal issues in the protection of children. *International Review of Law, Computers & Technology, 20*(1/2).177-185.doi:10.1080/13600860600579779

Natalie, L. (n.d). State of Michigan department of atty. general works to stop Internet predators. *Michigan Lawyers Weekly*

News 4, KVOA. (2012). *Town teen says Mass. man enticed sex acts over webcam.* Retrieved from http://www.kvoa.com

Nissley, E. (2008, March). Study shows Internet child predators not necessarily posing as teenagers. *Citizens' Voice.* Wilkes-Barre, Pa. p. T.26

Öztürk, E., & Özmen, S. (2011). An investigation of the problematic Internet use of teacher candidates based on personality types, shyness and demographic factors. *Educational Sciences: Theory & Practice, 11*(4). 1799-1808

Patterson, T. (2007). Child sex tourism. *FBI Law Enforcement Bulletin, 76*(1), 16-21. Retrieved from http://search.proquest.com/docview /204187369?accountid=27965

Pearse, J. (2009). Government catches up with industry's safety initiatives. *New Media Age*, 2

Pearson, M., Parkin, S., & Coomber, R. (2011). Generalizing applied qualitative research on harm reduction: The example of a public injecting typology. *Contemporary Drug Problems*, *38*(1). 61-91

Peter, J,. Valkenburg, P., Schouten, A., & Alexander P. (2005). Developing a model of adolescent friendship formation on the Internet. *CyberPsychology & Behavior*, *8*(5). 423-430. doi:10.1089/cpb.2005.8.423

Powell, A. (2010). Configuring consent: Emerging technologies, unauthorised sexual images and sexual assault. *Australian & New Zealand Journal of Criminology (Australian Academic Press)*. *43*(1), 76-90. doi:10.1375/acri.43.1.76

Preston, C. B. (2007). Zoning the Internet: A new approach to protecting children online. *Brigham Young University Law Review*, *2007*(6), 1417-1469

O'Grady, R. (2001). Eradicating pedophilia: Toward the humanization of society. *Journal of International Affairs*, *55*(1). 123-140. Retrieved from ABI/INFORM Global. (Document ID: 85559238)

Rambaree, K. (2008). Internet-mediated dating/romance of Mauritian early adolescents: A grounded theory analysis. *International Journal of Emerging Technologies & Society*, *6*(1), 34-59

Rep. Robert, C. S. (n.d). Rep. Robert C. Scott holds a hearing on online privacy and social networking. *FDCH Political Transcripts*

Salkind, N. (2003). *Exploring Research, 5e*. Prentice-Hall, Inc.

Shannon, D. (2008). Online sexual grooming in Sweden—Online and offline sex offences against children as described in Swedish police data. *Journal of Scandinavian Studies in Criminology & Crime Prevention*, *9*(2). 160-180. doi:10.1080/14043850802450120

Shank, G. (2002). *Qualitative research: A personal skills approach*. Upper Saddle River, NJ: Merrill, Prentice Hall

Shao, G. (2009). Understanding the appeal of user-generated media: A uses and gratification perspective. *Internet Research, 19*(1), 7-25. doi:10.1108/10662240910927795

Sharpe, C. A. (2009). *Methods used by internet predators to lure children into offline contact: How law enforcement and mental health professionals view grooming and assess risk*. The Chicago School of Professional Psychology. *ProQuest Dissertations and Theses,* http://search.proquest.com/docview/305140547?accoun tid=27965

Soster, R. L., & Drenten, J. M. (2010). Summary Brief: I'll show you mine, if you show me yours: Public policy implications of adolescent sexting. *Society for Marketing Advances Proceedings,* 114-115

Stanley, J. (2001). *Child abuse and the Internet*. Child Abuse Prevention Issues Number 15 Summer 2001, Australian Institute of Family Studies

Stathopulu, E., Hulse, J., & Canning, D. (2003). Difficulties with age estimation of Internet images of South-East Asian Girls. *Child Abuse Review, 12*(1). 46-57. doi:10.1002/car.781

Steinberger, C. (2009). Cyberspace: The nodal self in the wide wide world-adolescents signing-on. *Psychoanalytic Review, 96*(1). 129-144. Retrieved from MEDLINE with Full Text database

Subrahmanyam, K., Greenfield, P., & Tynes, (2004). Constructing sexuality and identity in an online teen chat room. *Journal of Applied Developmental Psychology, 25*(6), 651-666. ISSN 0193-3973, 10.1016/j.appdev.2004.09.007

Taylor, B. (2006). Online pervert who terrorized girls is jailed for 10 years. *Daily Mail*. 31

Taylor, R., Caeti, T., Loper, D., Fritsch, E., Liederbach, J. (2006). *Digital Crime and Digital Terrorism, 1e*. Pearson Education, Inc.

Thornburgh, D., & Herbert L. (2004). Youth, pornography, and the Internet. *Issues in Science and Technology*, 20(2). 43-48. Retrieved from Research Library. (Document ID: 536816021)

Valcke, M., Bonte, S., De Wever, B., & Rots, I. (2010). Internet parenting styles and the impact on Internet use of primary school children. *Computers & Education, 55* 454-464. doi:10.1016/j.compedu.2010.02.009

van den Eijnden, R., Spijkerman, R., Vermulst, A., van Rooij, T., & Engels, R. (2010). Compulsive internet use among adolescents: Bidirectional parent-child relationships. *Journal of Abnormal Child Psychology, 38*(1), 77-89

van Manen, M. (2010). The pedagogy of Momus technologies: Facebook, privacy, and online intimacy. *Qualitative Health Research, 20*(8), 1023-1032. ISSN 1049-7323, 08/2010

Vorauer, J. D., Cameron, J. J., Holmes, J. G., & Pearce, D. G. (2003). Invisible overtures: Fears of rejection and the signal amplification bias. *Journal of Personality and Social Psychology, 84*(4). 793-812. doi:10.1037/0022-3514.84.4.793

Wang, R., Bianchi, S., & Raley, S. (2005). Teenagers' Internet use and family rules: A research note. *Journal of Marriage & Family, 67*(5), 1249-1258. doi:10.1111/j.1741-3737.2005.00214.x

Welch, S. R. (2007). *Nightshift street ministries: Improving services to the homeless in Surrey*. (Masters thesis, Royal Roads University, 2007). Library and Archives Canada. (ISBN:978-0-494-27214-5)

Wells, M., & Mitchell, K. (2007). Youth sexual exploitation on the Internet: DSM-IV diagnoses and gender differences in co-occurring mental health issues. *Child & Adolescent Social Work Journal, 24*(3), 235-260. doi:10.1007/s10560-007-0083-z

Windmann, S., & Chmielewski, A. (2008). Emotion-induced modulation of recognition memory decisions in a go/nogo task: Response bias or memory bias? *Cognition & Emotion, 22*(5), 761-776. doi:10.1080/02699930701507899

Wolak, J., David, F., Mitchell, K., & Ybarra, M. (2008). Online "predators" and their victims: myths, realities, and implications for prevention treatment. *American Psychologist, 63*(2), 111-128. doi:10.1037/0003-066X.63.2.111

Wolfe, S., & Higgins, G. (2008). College students' punishment perceptions of online solicitation of children for sex. *American Journal of Criminal Justice, 33*(2), 193-208. doi:10.1007/s12103-008-9039-x

Wurtele, S. K., & Kenny, M. C. (2010). Preventing online sexual victimization of youth. *Journal of Behavior Analysis of Offender & Victim: Treatment & Prevention, 2*(1), 63-73

Informed Consent

UNIVERSITY OF PHOENIX
INFORMED CONSENT:
PARTICIPANTS 18 YEARS OF AGE AND OLDER

Dear _____ ,

My name is Rodney Alexander and I am a student at the University of Phoenix working on a doctoral degree. I am conducting a research study entitled How to Protect Children from Internet Predators. The purpose of the research study is to explore the causes of 13 to 17 year-old teenagers falling victim to child predators on the Internet.

Your participation will involve answering five questions related to your opinion on the teen Internet sexual assault phenomenon. Your participation in this study is voluntary. If you choose not to participate or to withdraw from the study at any time, you can do so without penalty or loss of benefit to yourself. The results of the research study may be published but your identity will remain confidential and your name will not be disclosed to any outside party.

In this research, there are no foreseeable risks to you.

Although there may be no direct benefit to you, a possible benefit of your participation is that more will be known about teen Internet sexual assault which may lead to better prevention methods.

If you have any questions concerning the research study, please call me at XXX-XXX-XXX and xxxx@xxx.com.

As a participant in this study, you could understand the following:

1. You may decline to participate or withdraw from participation at any time without consequences.
2. Your identity will be kept confidential.
3. Rodney Alexander the researcher has thoroughly explained the parameters of the research study and all of your questions and concerns have been addressed.
4. If the interviews are recorded, you must grant permission for the researcher, Rodney Alexander to digitally record the interview. You understand that the information from the recorded interviews may be transcribed. The researcher will structure a coding process to assure that anonymity of your name is protected.
5. Data will be stored in a secure and locked area. The data will be held for a period of three years, and then destroyed.
6. The research results will be used for publication.

"By signing this form you acknowledge that you understand the nature of the study, the potential risks to you as a participant, and the means by which your identity will be kept confidential. Your signature on this form also indicates that you are 18 years old or older and that you give your permission to voluntarily serve as a participant in the study described."

Signature of the interviewee _____

Date _____

Signature of the researcher _____

Date _____

Permission Letter to Use Premises

The permission from the School District was removed to Protect Its Identity

Interview Protocols

Interview Questions

A qualitative, phenomenological study is to allow the subject to share their experiences and have their voice heard. This study will follow that design, and will use questions to clarify or expand on points made by the subject. General, semi-structured, open-ended questions will be used for the interview questions to elicit personal feelings about the experience of how teens encounter sexual partners on the Internet. The numbered interview questions are not meant to guide the interview or direct responses, and the subset of questions are only for clarification purposes, if needed.

1. Please share with me your opinion on what circumstances most likely lead to teenage sexual encounters with someone whom they meet on the Internet?

2. Please share with me your opinion on how teenagers will most likely meet people on the Internet; for example, in a chat room, on MySpace™, on Facebook® or something totally different?

3. What role do you feel that a teen's personality; for example, A-introverted, B-extraverted or something totally different plays in whether they will meet a predator on the Internet?

   a. Do you feel that an introverted teen is more likely to attract a predator?

   b. Do you feel that an extroverted teen is more likely to attract a predator?

4. Please share with me your opinion on the role that teen gratification; for example, sex, companionship, self-esteem, or something else plays in whether a teen will meet an Internet predator?

5. Please share with me your opinion on what support would most likely help; for example, more parental supervision, better law enforcement, better High School curriculum or other to prevent teen's contact with an Internet Predator?

6. Demographic data

    a. Sex (male or female)

    b. Number of children

    c. Ethnicity

7. Would it be okay to contact you if there are follow on questions?

Transcripts of Participants' Interviews

Participant A Interview
Present during interview: Participant A and Researcher

Location of interview: High School in a Midwestern United States town

Date and time of interview: Thursday, February 02, 2012, 1:52 PM

Observation and comment:

INTERVIEW A
Researcher: I would like to conduct short 15-minute interview. The interview will consist of six open-ended questions designed to obtain your opinion on teenage (13 to 17 year-olds) sexual contact with someone whom they meet on the Internet. The interview is designed to learn more about the child's

possible motives and Internet tools used which led to the sexual contact. Finally, the interviews will explore potential solutions which could reduce the amount of teen sexual contact on the Internet. I have permission from the school district and the principal to conduct the interviews. You will be given a $15 Subway Restaurant Gift Certificate as thanks for participating in the interview.

Researcher: First question, please share with me your opinion on what circumstances most likely lead to teenage sexual encounters with someone whom they meet on the Internet?

Participant A: Our daughter had this pattern of behavior of looking to meet boys online because she was desperate to have a boyfriend. She had a significant history of meeting boys online through various online chat groups/social networks. Whenever we found out about the boys, we would block that chat group and educate our daughter on the dangers of meeting people online. She was very insistent that she would know the difference between a boy and a sexual predator. We tried numerous software to block access to certain sites, but she seemed to always find ways around the blocks. We started limiting her computer access and she was only allowed to use the computer in our presence, but she started getting up in the middle of the night to use the Wii to access the internet and stealing my cell phone to access the internet to chat with the man. She also gave him our phone number and when he would call he would block his number. We started randomly picking up the phone to listen in on her conversations but he would hang up and then he started calling in the middle of the night when we were asleep.

Our daughter is intelligent and she has Attention Deficit Hyperactivity Disorder (ADHD) which we feel added to her impulsivity and drive to find a boyfriend.

She was also raped by a boy (who she did not meet online) which seemed to escalate her drive to find an online boyfriend.

We also suspect that she fears rejection because her biological father signed away his parental rights when she was two, and has had no contact with her.

She has dreamed of finding him someday and that he would be able to explain why he signed away his rights and they would be able to establish a relationship again.

Researcher: Second question, please share with me your opinion on how teenagers will most likely meet people on the Internet; for example, in a chat room, on MySpace™, on Facebook® or something totally different?

Participant A: Our daughter used Facebook®, Yahoo chat rooms, Teenchat, MSN Messenger, Xat chat.

Researcher: Third question, what role do you feel that a teen's personality; for example, A-introverted, B-extroverted or something totally different plays in whether they will meet a predator on the Internet?

Participant A: Extroverted. We feel that her personality along with her ADHD, Post Traumatic Stress Disorder (PTSD), depression, and mood disorder played a role in her behavior. She is extremely extroverted. We have a daughter who is introverted and she does not seek relationships with boys, whereas our other daughter is very extroverted and has a very high interest in boys.

Researcher: Fourth question, please share with me your opinion on the role that teen gratification; for example, sex, companionship, self-esteem, or something else plays in whether a teen will meet an Internet predator?

Participant A: Our daughter was not looking for sex. She was looking for a boyfriend and someone that she could marry one day. She has low self-esteem, so these factors made her very easy to manipulate. She was very defiant in the home, but with the predator she was willing to do anything for him to make him happy because she was afraid of rejection. He did a great job of manipulating her feelings and weaknesses. He really got to know her and took on a parental role when it fit or was very "loving" towards her as a boyfriend.

Researcher: Fifth question, please share with me your opinion on what support would most likely help; for example, more parental supervision, better law enforcement, better High School curriculum or other to prevent teen's contact with an Internet Predator?

Participant A: We have cut off Internet access for our daughter for now. One parent is home at all times, but most of her interactions with the man took place after we went to bed. As soon as we found out we notified law enforcement, but they have been unable to trace the Internet Protocol (IP) addresses and he closed all accounts that he was using to interact with our daughter. We educated our daughter about the risks of the Internet and she has even sat with us to watch Chris Hansen's TV show *Catch a Predator*, as well as *Law and Order SVU* episodes involving children and sexual predators. It seems silly, but she was interested in watching these shows, so we used them as teaching moments.

She was very confident that she would be able to tell the difference between a boy and a sexual predator. She did not think it odd that the man she met originally presented himself as a 16 year-old boy and then eventually he told her he was 26. She thought it was great that an older man was interested in her, and he really exploited her low self-esteem by telling her how lucky he was to have met her, how beautiful she was, how she was much better than the women he worked with, etc.

I think adolescents respond well to peer groups. It has been unfortunate that our daughter has received mixed feedback regarding her interactions with this man. Some of her peers thought that it was great that she was involved with an older man and that he seemed to care so much for her, only a few peers told her that what she had done was stupid and she was lucky he did not kill her. I also think that adolescents need to experience in a controlled environment that they cannot tell the difference between a sexual predator and a boy. They never seem to take an adults advice, but if they experience for themselves it seems to have more of an impact.

Researcher: Sixth question, please share with me your demographic data (sex, number of children, ethnicity).

Participant A: Female/5/Caucasian.

Researcher: Last question, would it be okay to contact you if there are follow on questions?

Participant A: Yes.

Participant B Interview

Present during interview: Participant B and Researcher

Location of interview: Midtown USA High School

Date and time of interview: Thursday, February 02, 2012, 2:15 PM

Observation and comment:

INTERVIEW B

Researcher: I would like to conduct short 15-minute interview. The interview will consist of six open-ended questions designed to obtain your opinion on teenage (13 to 17 year-olds) sexual contact with someone whom they meet on the Internet. The interview is designed to learn more about the child's possible motives and Internet tools used which led to the sexual contact. Finally, the interview will explore potential solutions which could reduce the amount of teen sexual contact on the Internet. I have permission from the school district and the principal to conduct the interviews. You will be given a $15 Subway Restaurant Gift Certificate as thanks for participating in the interview.

Researcher: First question, please share with me your opinion on what circumstances most likely lead to teenage sexual encounters with someone whom they meet on the Internet?

Participant B: Using websites like Facebook® and Twitter© or cell phones.

Researcher: Second question, please share with me your opinion on how teenagers will most likely meet people on the Internet; for example, in a chat room, on MySpace™, on Facebook® or something totally different?

Participant B: Twitter© and Facebook® - Most accessible on cell phones.

Researcher: Third question, what role do you feel that a teen's personality; for example, A-introverted, B-extroverted or something totally different plays in whether they will meet a predator on the Internet?

Participant B: Extroverted. Rebelling against traditional family structure and values.

Researcher: Fourth question, please share with me your opinion on the role that teen gratification; for example, sex, companionship, self-esteem, or something else plays in whether a teen will meet an Internet predator?

Participant B: Idea of forbidden fruit - Outside the norm/exploring boundaries/rebelling.

Researcher: Fifth question, please share with me your

opinion on what support would most likely help; for example, more parental supervision, better law enforcement, better High School curriculum or other to prevent teen's contact with an Internet Predator?

Participant B: Significant adults in their lives – not classes, affect Teens.

Researcher: Sixth question, please share with me your demographic data (sex, number of children, ethnicity).

Participant B: Male/2/American.

Researcher: Last question, would it be okay to contact you if there are follow on questions?

Participant B: Yes.

Participant C Interview

Present during interview: Participant C and Researcher

Location of interview: Midwestern USA High School

Date and time of interview: Thursday, February 02, 2012, 2:28 PM

Observation and comment:

INTERVIEW C

Researcher: I would like to conduct short 15-minute interview. The interview will consist of six open-ended questions designed to obtain your opinion on teenage (13 to 17 year-olds) sexual contact with someone whom they meet on the Internet. The interview is designed to learn more about the child's possible motives and Internet tools used that led to the sexual contact. Finally, the interview will explore potential solutions that could reduce the amount of teen sexual contact on the Internet. I have permission from the school district and the principal to conduct the interviews. You will be given a $15 Subway Restaurant Gift Certificate as thanks for participating in the interview.

Researcher: First question, please share with me your opinion on what circumstances most likely lead to teenage sexual encounters with someone whom they meet on the Internet?

Participant C: Students who cannot form relationships at school/rebelling against parents.

Researcher: Second question, please share with me your opinion on how teenagers will most likely meet people on the Internet; for example, in a chat room, on MySpace™, on Facebook® or something totally different?

Participant C: Facebook® and Twitter© - easily accessible or possibly Craig's List.

Researcher: Third question, what role do you feel that a teen's personality; for example, A-introverted, B-extroverted or something totally different plays in whether they will meet a predator on the Internet?

Participant C: A. Insecurity - Looking for acceptance in other places.

Researcher: Fourth question, please share with me your opinion on the role that teen gratification; for example, sex, companionship, self-esteem, or something else plays in whether a teen will meet an Internet predator?

Participant C: Immediate gratification - having the adult relationship that they see on TV.

Researcher: Fifth question, please share with me your

opinion on what support would most likely help; for example, more parental supervision, better law enforcement, better High School curriculum, or other) to teen's your contact with an Internet Predator?

Participant C: Educating kids about risks- Parents monitoring internet activity.

Researcher: Sixth question, please share with me your demographic data (sex, number of children, ethnicity).

Participant C: Male/0/Caucasian.

Researcher: Last question, would it be okay to contact you if there are follow on questions?

Participant C: Yes.

Participant D Interview

Present during interview: Participant D and Researcher

Location of interview: Midwestern United States town High School

Date and time of interview: Thursday, February 02, 2012, 3:47 PM

Observation and comment:

INTERVIEW D

Researcher: I would like to conduct short 15-minute interview. The interview will consist of six open-ended questions designed to obtain your opinion on teenage (13 to 17 year-olds) sexual contact with someone whom they meet on the Internet. The interview is designed to learn more about the child's possible motives and Internet tools used that led to the sexual contact. Finally, the interview will explore potential solutions which could reduce the amount of teen sexual contact on the Internet. I have permission from the school district and the principal to conduct the interviews. You will be given a $15 Subway Restaurant Gift Certificate as thanks for participating in the interview.

Researcher: First question, please share with me your opinion on what circumstances most likely lead to teenage sexual encounters with someone whom they meet on the Internet?

Participant D: Dysfunctional families and lack of caring environment in the home.

Researcher: Second question, please share with me your opinion on how teenagers will most likely meet people on the Internet; for example, in a chat room, on MySpace™, on Facebook® or something totally different?

Participant D: All are easily open and accessible to students - particularly newer sites.

Researcher: Third question, what role do you feel that a teen's personality; for example, A-introverted, B-extroverted or something totally different plays in whether they will meet a predator on the Internet?

Participant D: Both introverted and extroverted - They will both try to reach out in diff. ways if they feel a void

Researcher: Fourth question, please share with me your opinion on the role that teen gratification; for example, sex, companionship, self-esteem, or something else plays in whether a teen will meet an Internet predator?

Participant D: Instant response that Internet provides.

Researcher: Fifth question, please share with me your

opinion on what support would most likely help; for example, more parental supervision, better law enforcement, better High School curriculum or other to prevent teen's contact with an Internet Predator?

Participant D: Curriculum - Students are relying on peers for info and it is uninformed.

Researcher: Sixth question, please share with me your demographic data (sex, number of children, ethnicity).

Participant D: Female/2/Caucasian.

Researcher: Last question, would it be okay to contact you if there are follow on questions?

Participant D: Yes.

Participant E Interview

Present during interview: Participant E and Researcher

Location of interview: Midwestern United States town High School

Date and time of interview: Thursday, February 02, 2012, 3:56 PM

Observation and comment:

INTERVIEW E

Researcher: I would like to conduct short 15-minute interview. The interview will consist of six open-ended questions designed to obtain your opinion on teenage (13 to 17 year-olds) sexual contact with someone whom they meet on the Internet. The interview is designed to learn more about the child's possible motives and Internet tools used which led to the sexual contact. Finally, the interview will explore potential solutions which could reduce the amount of teen sexual contact on the Internet. I have permission from the school district and the principal to conduct the interviews. You will be given a $15 Subway Restaurant Gift Certificate as thanks for participating in the interview.

Researcher: First question, please share with me your opinion on what circumstances most likely lead to teenage sexual encounters with someone whom they meet on the Internet?

Participant E: Social networking.

Researcher: Second question, please share with me your opinion on how teenagers will most likely meet people on the Internet; for example in a chat room, on MySpace™, on Facebook®, or something totally different?

Participant J: Social networking websites - they are more interactive and very popular.

Researcher: Third question, what role do you feel that a teen's personality; for example, A-introverted, B-extroverted or something totally different plays in whether they will meet a predator on the Internet?

Participant E: B; they are more outgoing and have a desire to meet people.

Researcher: Fourth question, please share with me your opinion on the role that teen gratification; for example, sex, companionship, self-esteem, or something else plays in whether a teen will meet an Internet predator?

Participant E: Desire to be accepted and meet people.

Researcher: Fifth question, please share with me your opinion on what support would most likely help; for example, more parental supervision, better law

enforcement, better High School curriculum or other to prevent teen's contact with an Internet Predator?

Participant E: More community education and awareness and parental supervision.

Researcher: Sixth question, please share with me your demographic data (sex, number of children, ethnicity).

Participant E: Male/1/Caucasian and Hispanic.

Researcher: Last question, would it be okay to contact you if there are follow on questions?

Participant E: Yes.

Participant F Interview

Present during interview: Participant F and Researcher

Location of interview: Midwestern United States town High School

Date and time of interview: Thursday, February 02, 2012, 4:09 PM

Observation and comment:

INTERVIEW F

Researcher: I would like to conduct short 15-minute interviews. The interview will consist of six open-ended questions designed to obtain your opinion on teenage (13 to 17 year-olds) sexual contact with someone whom they meet on the Internet. The interview is designed to learn more about the child's possible motives and Internet tools used which led to the sexual contact. Finally, the interview will explore potential solutions which could reduce the amount of teen sexual contact on the Internet. I have permission from the school district and the principal to conduct the interviews. You will be given a $15 Subway Restaurant Gift Certificate as thanks for participating in the interview.

Researcher: First question, please share with me your opinion on what circumstances most likely lead to teenage sexual encounters with someone whom they meet on the Internet?

Participant F: Inappropriate use of social media - Photos/info with no blocks/unsupervised.

Researcher: Second question, please share with me your opinion on how teenagers will most likely meet people on the Internet; for example, in a chat room, on MySpace™, on Facebook® or something totally different?

Participant F: Facebook® and Twitter© as well as some chat rooms.

Researcher: Third question, what role do you feel that a teen's personality; for example, A-introverted, B-extroverted or something totally different plays in whether they will meet a predator on the Internet?

Participant F: Both - Introvert wants someone to connect with/can be someone they are not.

Researcher: Fourth question, please share with me your opinion on the role that teen gratification; for example, sex, companionship, self-esteem, or something else plays in whether a teen will meet an Internet predator?

Participant F: Need for contact is the biggest thing. The shy teen wants connection.

Researcher: Fifth question, please share with me your

opinion on what support would most likely help; for example, more parental supervision, better law enforcement, better High School curriculum or other to prevent teen's contact with an Internet Predator?

Participant F: Parental support and connections in school - Parents need to know.

Researcher: Sixth question, please share with me your demographic data (sex, number of children, ethnicity).

Participant F: Female/2/Caucasian.

Researcher: Last question, would it be okay to contact you if there are follow on questions?

Participant F: Yes.

Participant G Interview

Present during interview: Participant G and Researcher

Location of interview: Midwestern United States town High School

Date and time of interview: Friday, February 03, 2012, 11:26 AM

Observation and comment:

Interview G

Researcher: I would like to conduct short 15-minute interview. The interview will consist of six open-ended questions designed to obtain your opinion on teenage (13 to 17 year-olds) sexual contact with someone whom they meet on the Internet. The interview is designed to learn more about the child's possible motives and Internet tools used which led to the sexual contact. Finally, the interview will explore potential solutions which could reduce the amount of teen sexual contact on the Internet. I have permission from the school district and the principal to conduct the interview. You will be given a $15 Subway Restaurant Gift Certificate as thanks for participating in the interview.

Researcher: First question, please share with me your opinion on what circumstances most likely lead to teenage sexual encounters with someone whom they meet on the Internet?

Participant G: Student is not monitored - family is not interactive with child.

Researcher: Second question, please share with me your opinion on how teenagers will most likely meet people on the Internet; for example, in a chat room, on MySpace™, on Facebook® or something totally different?

Participant G: Chat rooms - Anyone can use them. On Facebook® you have to accept friendships.

Researcher: Third question, what role do you feel that a teen's personality; for example, A-introverted, B-extroverted or something totally different plays in whether they will meet a predator on the Internet?

Participant G: A - Feel they cannot talk face to face so are more apt to reach out online. Researcher: Fourth question, please share with me your opinion on the role that teen gratification; for example, sex, companionship, self-esteem, or something else plays in whether a teen will meet an Internet predator?

Participant G: This is the only way they would be receiving feedback and it's accessible.

Researcher: Fifth question, please share with me your opinion on what support would most likely help; for example, more parental supervision, better law

enforcement, better High School curriculum or other to prevent teen's contact with an Internet Predator?

Participant G: Parental/adult supervision - Someone who cares for the child.

Researcher: Sixth question, please share with me your demographic data (sex, number of children, ethnicity).

Participant G: Female/3/Hawaiian.

Researcher: Last question, would it be okay to contact you if there are follow on questions?

Participant G: Yes.

Participant H Interview

Present during interview: Participant H and Researcher

Location of interview: Midwestern United States town High School

Date and time of interview: Friday, February 03, 2012, 12:03 PM

Observation and comment:

INTERVIEW H

Researcher: I would like to conduct short 15-minute interview. The interview will consist of six open-ended questions designed to obtain your opinion on teenage (13 to 17 year-olds) sexual contact with someone whom they meet on the Internet. The interview is designed to learn more about the child's possible motives and Internet tools used which led to the sexual contact. Finally the interviews will explore potential solutions which could reduce the amount of teen sexual contact on the Internet. I have permission from the school district and the principal to conduct the interviews. You will be given a $15 Subway Restaurant Gift Certificate as thanks for participating in the interviews.

Researcher: First question, please share with me your opinion on what circumstances most likely lead to teenage sexual encounters with someone whom they meet on the Internet?

Participant H: Loneliness and a wish to connect/low self-esteem/no parental guidance.

Researcher: Second question, please share with me your opinion on how teenagers will most likely meet people on the Internet; for example, in a chat room, on MySpace™, on Facebook® or something totally different?

Participant H: Facebook® is the most popular/used the most. Craigslist is unmonitored.

Researcher: Third question, what role do you feel that a teen's personality; for example, A-introverted, B-extroverted or something totally different plays in whether they will meet a predator on the Internet?

Participant H: Has to do more with wanting to have fun and wanting to conform and explore.

Researcher: Fourth question, please share with me your opinion on the role that teen gratification; for example, sex, companionship, self-esteem, or something else plays in whether a teen will meet an Internet predator?

Participant H: Self-esteem/Wanting to be accepted by people who they think are friends.

Researcher: Fifth question, please share with me your

opinion on what support would most likely help; for example, more parental supervision, better law enforcement, better High School curriculum or other to prevent teen's contact with an Internet Predator?

Participant H: Parental supervision - Kids will do what they want on the internet.

Researcher: Sixth question, please share with me your demographic data (sex, number of children, ethnicity).

Participant H: Female/1/Caucasian.

Researcher: Last question, would it be okay to contact you if there are follow on questions?

Participant H: Yes, if it is short.

Participant I Interview

Present during interview: Participant I and Researcher

Location of interview: Midwestern United States town High School

Date and time of interview: Friday, February 03, 2012, 12:19 PM

Observation and comment:

INTERVIEW I

Researcher: I would like to conduct short 15-minute interview. The interview will consist of six open-ended questions designed to obtain your opinion on teenage (13 to 17 year-olds) sexual contact with someone whom they meet on the Internet. The interview is designed to learn more about the child's possible motives and Internet tools used which led to the sexual contact. Finally the interviews will explore potential solutions which could reduce the amount of teen sexual contact on the Internet. I have permission from the school district and the principal to conduct the interviews. You will be given a $15 Subway Restaurant Gift Certificate as thanks for participating in the interviews.

Researcher: First question, please share with me your opinion on what circumstances most likely lead to teenage sexual encounters with someone whom they meet on the Internet?

Participant I: Identity of the person not being revealed.

Researcher: Second question, please share with me your opinion on how teenagers will most likely meet people on the Internet; for example, in a chat room, on MySpace™, on Facebook® or something totally different?

Participant I: Facebook® - Contact has children that are on Facebook® all the time.

Researcher: Third question, what role do you feel that a teen's personality; for example, A-introverted, B-extroverted or something totally different plays in whether they will meet a predator on the Internet?

Participant I: Lonely - They would respond to friend of a friend on Facebook®.

Researcher: Fourth question, please share with me your opinion on the role that teen gratification; for example, sex, companionship, self-esteem, or something else plays in whether a teen will meet an Internet predator?

Participant I: Self-esteem/Desire to be loved/ Adventure/Doing what they see in movies.

Researcher: Fifth question, please share with me your opinion on what support would most likely help; for

example, more parental supervision, better law en-forcement, better High School curriculum or other to prevent teen's contact with an Internet Predator?

Participant I: Less time on Facebook®/More interaction and social groups away from the computer.

Researcher: Sixth question, please share with me your demographic data (sex, number of children, ethnicity).

Participant I: Female/4/Anglo.

Researcher: Last question, would it be okay to contact you if there are follow on questions?

Participant I: Yes.

Participant J Interview

Present during interview: Participant J and Researcher

Location of interview: Transitional housing office area

Date and time of interview: Friday, February 03, 2012, 12:30 PM

Observation and comment:

INTERVIEW J

Researcher: I would like to conduct short 15-minute interview. The interview will consist of six open-ended questions designed to obtain your opinion on teenage (13 to 17 year-olds) sexual contact with someone whom they meet on the Internet. The interview is designed to learn more about the child's possible motives and Internet tools used which led to the sexual contact. Finally, the interview will explore potential solutions which could reduce the amount of teen sexual contact on the Internet. I have permission from the school district and the principal to conduct the interviews. You will be given a $15 Subway Restaurant Gift Certificate as thanks for participating in the interview.

Researcher: First question, please share with me your opinion on what circumstances most likely lead to teenage sexual encounters with someone whom they meet on the Internet?

Participant J: Loneliness/They want to behave as adults but do not have parental guidance.

Researcher: Second question, please share with me your opinion on how teenagers will most likely meet people on the Internet; for example, in a chat room, on MySpace™, on Facebook® or something totally different?

Participant J: All of the above/Friends/Perusing the internet without supervision.

Researcher: Third question, what role do you feel that a teen's personality; for example, A-introverted, B-extroverted or something totally different plays in whether they will meet a predator on the Internet?

Participant J: A or B - Depends on what is going on in student's life.

Researcher: Fourth question, please share with me your opinion on the role that teen gratification; for example, sex, companionship, self-esteem, or something else plays in whether a teen will meet an Internet predator?

Participant J: Feeling needed and wanted especially for females/What they see in media.

Researcher: Fifth question, please share with me your

opinion on what support would most likely help; for example, more parental supervision, better law enforcement, better High School curriculum or other to prevent teen's contact with an Internet Predator?

Participant J: Parental supervision/Active and engaging after school programs.

Researcher: Sixth question, please share with me your demographic data (sex, number of children, ethnicity).

Participant J: Female/0/Caucasian.

Researcher: Last question, would it be okay to contact you if there are follow on questions?

Participant J: Yes.

Participant K Interview

Present during interview: Participant K and Researcher

Location of interview: Midwestern United States town High School

Date and time of interview: Friday, February 03, 2012, 1:17 PM

Observation and comment:

INTERVIEW K

Researcher: I would like to conduct short 15-minute interview. The interview will consist of six open-ended questions designed to obtain your opinion on teenage (13 to 17 year-olds) sexual contact with someone whom they meet on the Internet. The interview is designed to learn more about the child's possible motives and Internet tools used which led to the sexual contact. Finally, the interview will explore potential solutions which could reduce the amount of teen sexual contact on the Internet. I have permission from the school district and the principal to conduct the interviews. You will be given a $15 Subway Restaurant Gift Certificate as thanks for participating in the interview.

Researcher: First question, please share with me your opinion on what circumstances most likely lead to teenage sexual encounters with someone whom they meet on the Internet?

Participant K: Access to internet throughout day/no supervision/cannot verify individuals

Researcher: Second question, please share with me your opinion on how teenagers will most likely meet people on the Internet; for example, in a chat room, on MySpace™, on Facebook® or something totally different?

Participant K: Chat room - More open where Facebook® has more control.

Researcher: Third question, what role do you feel that a teen's personality; for example, A-introverted, B-extroverted or something totally different plays in whether they will meet a predator on the Internet?

Participant K: A - Looking for relationships/more susceptible to what others say online.

Researcher: Fourth question, please share with me your opinion on the role that teen gratification; for example, sex, companionship, self-esteem, or something else plays in whether a teen will meet an Internet predator?

Participant K: Communication - someone to have a relationship with.

Researcher: Fifth question, please share with me your

opinion on what support would most likely help; for example, more parental supervision, better law enforcement, better High School curriculum, or other to prevent a teen's contact with an Internet Predator?

Participant K: Combination of each - supervising what kids are doing online.

Participant K: Female/1/Caucasian.

Researcher: Sixth question, please share with me your demographic data (sex, number of children, ethnicity).

Researcher: Last question, would it be okay to contact you if there are follow on questions?

Participant K: Yes.

Participant L Interview

Present during interview: Participant L and Researcher

Location of interview: Midwestern United States town High School

Date and time of interview: Friday, February 03, 2012, 2:04 PM

Observation and comment:

INTERVIEW L

Researcher: I would like to conduct short 15-minute interview. The interview will consist of six open-ended questions designed to obtain your opinion on teenage (13 to 17 year-olds) sexual contact with someone whom they meet on the Internet. The interview is designed to learn more about the child's possible motives and Internet tools used which led to the sexual contact. Finally, the interview will explore potential solutions which could reduce the amount of teen sexual contact on the Internet. I have permission from the school district and the principal to conduct the interviews. You will be given a $15 Subway Restaurant Gift Certificate as thanks for participating in the interview.

Researcher: First question, please share with me your opinion on what circumstances most likely lead to teenage sexual encounters with someone whom they meet on the Internet?

Participant L: Kids hide what they are doing on internet - Contact does not use it.

Researcher: Second question, please share with me your opinion on how teenagers will most likely meet people on the Internet; for example, in a chat room, on MySpace™, on Facebook® or something totally different?

Participant L: All of the above.

Researcher: Third question, what role do you feel that a teen's personality; for example, A-introverted, B-extroverted or something totally different plays in whether they will meet a predator on the Internet?

Participant L: A - They may be afraid of public rejection so this is their private world.

Researcher: Fourth question, please share with me your opinion on the role that teen gratification; for example, sex, companionship, self-esteem, or something else plays in whether a teen will meet an Internet predator?

Participant L: Children seem to value acceptance from peers more than family values.

Researcher: Fifth question, please share with me your opinion on what support would most likely help; for

example, more parental supervision, better law enforcement, better High School curriculum or other to prevent teen's contact with an Internet Predator?

Participant L: Law Enforcement - Parents are always last to know/Kids have hidden lives.

Researcher: Sixth question, please share with me your demographic data (sex, number of children, ethnicity).

Participant L: Female/0/African-American.

Researcher: Last question, would it be okay to contact you if there are follow on questions?

Participant L: Yes.

Participant M Interview

Present during interview: Participant M and Researcher

Location of interview: Midwestern United States town High School

Date and time of interview: Friday, February 03, 2012, 2:11 PM

Observation and comment:

INTERVIEW M

Researcher: I would like to conduct short 15-minute interview. The interview will consist of six open-ended questions designed to obtain your opinion on teenage (13 to 17 year-olds) sexual contact with someone whom they meet on the Internet. The interview is designed to learn more about the child's possible motives and Internet tools used which led to the sexual contact. Finally, the interview will explore potential solutions which could reduce the amount of teen sexual contact on the Internet. I have permission from the school district and the principal to conduct the interviews. You will be given a $15 Subway Restaurant Gift Certificate as thanks for participating in the interview.

Researcher: First question, please share with me your opinion on what circumstances most likely lead to teenage sexual encounters with someone whom they meet on the Internet?

Participant M: Lacking parent supervision/No one to be a guide in their lives.

Researcher: Second question, please share with me your opinion on how teenagers will most likely meet people on the Internet; for example, in a chat room, on MySpace™, on Facebook® or something totally different?

Participant M: Facebook® - It's the website they use the most.

Researcher: Third question, what role do you feel that a teen's personality; for example, A-introverted, B-extroverted or something totally different plays in whether they will meet a predator on the Internet?

Participant M: Students who are shyer would not get involved.

Researcher: Fourth question, please share with me your opinion on the role that teen gratification; for example, sex, companionship, self-esteem, or something else plays in whether a teen will meet an Internet predator?

Participant M: If students do not have friends they will be looking elsewhere for some.

Researcher: Fifth question, please share with me your

opinion on what support would most likely help; for example, more parental supervision, better law enforcement, better High School curriculum or other to prevent teen's contact with an Internet Predator?

Participant M: Parental supervision is key/In school there is teacher supervision.

Researcher: Sixth question, please share with me your demographic data (sex, number of children, ethnicity).

Participant M: Female/0/Hispanic.

Researcher: Last question, would it be okay to contact you if there are follow on questions?

Participant M: Yes, outside of school times.

Participant N Interview

Present during interview: Participant N and Researcher

Location of interview: Midwestern United States town High School

Date and time of interview: Friday, February 03, 2012, 2:21 PM

Observation and comment:

INTERVIEW N

Researcher: I would like to conduct short 15-minute interview. The interview will consist of six open-ended questions designed to obtain your opinion on teenage (13 to 17 year-olds) sexual contact with someone whom they meet on the Internet. The interview is designed to learn more about the child's possible motives and Internet tools used which led to the sexual contact. Finally, the interview will explore potential solutions which could reduce the amount of teen sexual contact on the Internet. I have permission from the school district and the principal to conduct the interviews. You will be given a $15 Subway Restaurant Gift Certificate as thanks for participating in the interview.

Researcher: First question, please share with me your opinion on what circumstances most likely lead to teenage sexual encounters with someone whom they meet on the Internet?

Participant N: Opportunity/Lack of parental guidance.

Researcher: Second question, please share with me your opinion on how teenagers will most likely meet people on the Internet; for example, in a chat room, on MySpace™, on Facebook® or something totally different?

Participant N: Facebook®.

Researcher: Third question, what role do you feel that a teen's personality; for example, A-introverted, B-extroverted or something totally different plays in whether they will meet a predator on the Internet?

Participant N: Personality may not have to do with it/ If receiving attention will respond.

Researcher: Fourth question, please share with me your opinion on the role that teen gratification; for example, sex, companionship, self-esteem, or something else plays in whether a teen will meet an Internet predator?

Participant N: Self-esteem - If they are looking for someone to validate them.

Researcher: Fifth question, please share with me your opinion on what support would most likely help; for example, more parental supervision, better law

enforcement, better High School curriculum or other to prevent teen's contact with an Internet Predator?

Participant N: Combination of parental guidance and Peer influence.

Researcher: Sixth question, please share with me your demographic data (sex, number of children, ethnicity).

Participant N: Female/0/Caucasian.

Researcher: Last question, would it be okay to contact you if there are follow on questions?

Participant N: Yes.

Participant O Interview

Present during interview: Participant O and Researcher

Location of interview: Midwestern United States town High School

Date and time of interview: Friday, February 03, 2012, 2:29 PM

Observation and comment:

INTERVIEW O

Researcher: I would like to conduct short 15-minute interview. The interview will consist of six open-ended questions designed to obtain your opinion on teenage (13 to 17 year-olds) sexual contact with someone whom they meet on the Internet. The interview is designed to learn more about the child's possible motives and Internet tools used which led to the sexual contact. Finally, the interview will explore potential solutions which could reduce the amount of teen sexual contact on the Internet. I have permission from the school district and the principal to conduct the interviews. You will be given a $15 Subway Restaurant Gift Certificate as thanks for participating in the interview.

Researcher: First question, please share with me your opinion on what circumstances most likely lead to teenage sexual encounters with someone whom they meet on the Internet?

Participant O: Feel safer since they are not talking to someone face to face.

Researcher: Second question, please share with me your opinion on how teenagers will most likely meet people on the Internet; for example, in a chat room, on MySpace™, on Facebook® or something totally different?

Participant O: MySpace™ and Facebook® - Social networks that anyone has access to.

Researcher: Third question, what role do you feel that a teen's personality; for example, A-introverted, B-extroverted or something totally different plays in whether they will meet a predator on the Internet?

Participant O: Personality does not really matter.

Researcher: Fourth question, please share with me your opinion on the role that teen gratification; for example, sex, companionship, self-esteem, or something else plays in whether a teen will meet an Internet predator?

Participant O: Huge factor if they are searching for it and meet a predator.

Researcher: Fifth question, please share with me your opinion on what support would most likely help; for

example, more parental supervision, better law enforcement, better High School curriculum or other to prevent teen's contact with an Internet Predator?

Participant O: Combination of parent supervision and internet safety tips in school.

Researcher: Sixth question, please share with me your demographic data (sex, number of children, ethnicity).

Participant O: Female/0/African-American.

Researcher: Last question, would it be okay to contact you if there are follow on questions?

Participant O: Yes.

Participant P Interview

Present during interview: Participant P and Researcher

Location of interview: Midwestern United States town High School

Date and time of interview: Friday, February 03, 2012, 2:47 PM

Observation and comment:

INTERVIEW P

Researcher: I would like to conduct short 15-minute interview. The interview will consist of six open-ended questions designed to obtain your opinion on teenage (13 to 17 year-olds) sexual contact with someone whom they meet on the Internet. The interview is designed to learn more about the child's possible motives and Internet tools used which led to the sexual contact. Finally, the interview will explore potential solutions which could reduce the amount of teen sexual contact on the Internet. I have permission from the school district and the principal to conduct the interviews. You will be given a $15 Subway Restaurant Gift Certificate as thanks for participating in the interview.

Researcher: First question, please share with me your opinion on what circumstances most likely lead to teenage sexual encounters with someone whom they meet on the Internet?

Participant P: Inexperience/Lack of knowledge/ Finding someone they think they can trust.

Researcher: Second question, please share with me your opinion on how teenagers will most likely meet people on the Internet; for example, in a chat room, on MySpace™, on Facebook® or something totally different?

Participant P: All of the above/Social Media/Twitter©/ any chance to communicate ideas.

Researcher: Third question, what role do you feel that a teen's personality; for example, A-introverted, B-extroverted or something totally different plays in whether they will meet a predator on the Internet?

Participant P: Both - Not one type of teen is more susceptible to predators.

Researcher: Fourth question, please share with me your opinion on the role that teen gratification; for example, sex, companionship, self-esteem, or something else plays in whether a teen will meet an Internet predator?

Participant P: Everyone acts based on what they need/ want but everyone acts differently.

Researcher: Fifth question, please share with me your

opinion on what support would most likely help; for example, more parental supervision, better law enforcement, better High School curriculum or other to prevent teen's contact with an Internet Predator?

Participant P: Relationship with someone that they trust and who will guide them.

Researcher: Sixth question, please share with me your demographic data (sex, number of children, ethnicity).

Participant P: Male/0/Caucasian.

Researcher: Last question, would it be okay to contact you if there are follow on questions?

Participant P: Yes.

Participant Q Interview

Present during interview: Participant Q and Researcher

Location of interview: Midwestern United States town High School

Date and time of interview: Friday, February 03, 2012, 3:42 PM

Observation and comment:

INTERVIEW Q

Researcher: I would like to conduct short 15-minute interview. The interview will consist of six open-ended questions designed to obtain your opinion on teenage (13 to 17 year-olds) sexual contact with someone whom they meet on the Internet. The interview is designed to learn more about the child's possible motives and Internet tools used which led to the sexual contact. Finally, the interview will explore potential solutions which could reduce the amount of teen sexual contact on the Internet. I have permission from the school district and the principal to conduct the interviews. You will be given a $15 Subway Restaurant Gift Certificate as thanks for participating in the interview.

Researcher: First question, please share with me your opinion on what circumstances most likely lead to teenage sexual encounters with someone whom they meet on the Internet?

Participant Q: Shy in social situations - this keeps them at a distance/Curiosity/Anonymity

Researcher: Second question, please share with me your opinion on how teenagers will most likely meet people on the Internet; for example, in a chat room, on MySpace™, on Facebook® or something totally different?

Participant Q: All of the above/Kids know more about technology than adults.

Researcher: Third question, what role do you feel that a teen's personality; for example, A-introverted, B-extroverted or something totally different plays in whether they will meet a predator on the Internet?

Participant Q: Possibly A but teens feel impervious/ either could be easily manipulated.

Researcher: Fourth question, please share with me your opinion on the role that teen gratification; for example, sex, companionship, self-esteem, or some-thing else plays in whether a teen will meet an Internet predator?

Participant Q: Growing up too early/immune to bom-bardment of sex in media/lower culture.

Researcher: Fifth question, please share with me your

opinion on what support would most likely help; for example, more parental supervision, better law enforcement, better High School curriculum or other to prevent teen's contact with an Internet Predator?

Participant Q: Parents need to make sure kids are secure/fit into environment.

Researcher: Sixth question, please share with me your demographic data (sex, number of children, ethnicity).

Participant Q: Male/0/Caucasian.

Researcher: Last question, would it be okay to contact you if there are follow on questions?

Participant Q: Yes.

Participant R Interview

Present during interview: Participant R and Researcher

Location of interview: Midwestern United States town High School

Date and time of interview: Friday, February 03, 2012, 3:53 PM

Observation and comment:

INTERVIEW R

Researcher: I would like to conduct short 15-minute interview. The interview will consist of six open-ended questions designed to obtain your opinion on teenage (13 to 17 year-olds) sexual contact with someone whom they meet on the Internet. The interview is designed to learn more about the child's possible motives and Internet tools used which led to the sexual contact. Finally, the interview will explore potential solutions which could reduce the amount of teen sexual contact on the Internet. I have permission from the school district and the principal to conduct the interviews. You will be given a $15 Subway Restaurant Gift Certificate as thanks for participating in the interview.

Researcher: First question, please share with me your opinion on what circumstances most likely lead to teenage sexual encounters with someone whom they meet on the Internet?

Participant R: When predator acts like a teenager - they would be sympathetic to problems.

Researcher: Second question, please share with me your opinion on how teenagers will most likely meet people on the Internet; for example, in a chat room, on MySpace™, on Facebook® or something totally different?

Participant R: Facebook® - Seems to be the most popular website.

Researcher: Third question, what role do you feel that a teen's personality; for example, A-introverted, B-extroverted or something totally different plays in whether they will meet a predator on the Internet?

Participant R: A - They have not talked with people in the community/they want attention.

Researcher: Fourth question, please share with me your opinion on the role that teen gratification; for example, sex, companionship, self-esteem, or something else plays in whether a teen will meet an Internet predator?

Participant R: Peer pressure/Kids exaggerate about what they do - some kids will believe it.

Researcher: Fifth question, please share with me your

opinion on what support would most likely help; for example, more parental supervision, better law enforcement, better High School curriculum or other to prevent teen's contact with an Internet Predator?

Participant R: Parental supervision and special courses in school.

Researcher: Sixth question, please share with me your demographic data (sex, number of children, ethnicity).

Participant R: Male/2/Caucasian.

Researcher: Last question, would it be okay to contact you if there are follow on questions?

Participant R: Yes.

Participant S Interview

Present during interview: Participant S and Researcher

Location of interview: Midwestern United States town High School

Date and time of interview: Monday, February 06, 2012, 1:22 PM

Observation and comment:

INTERVIEW S

Researcher: I would like to conduct short 15-minute interview. The interview will consist of six open-ended questions designed to obtain your opinion on teenage (13 to 17 year-olds) sexual contact with someone whom they meet on the Internet. The interview is designed to learn more about the child's possible motives and Internet tools used which led to the sexual contact. Finally, the interview will explore potential solutions which could reduce the amount of teen sexual contact on the Internet. I have permission from the school district and the principal to conduct the interviews. You will be given a $15 Subway Restaurant Gift Certificate as thanks for participating in the interview.

Researcher: First question, please share with me your opinion on what circumstances most likely lead to teenage sexual encounters with someone whom they meet on the Internet?

Participant S: Lack of parental controls/Lack of aware-ness of what their kids are doing.

Researcher: Second question, please share with me your opinion on how teenagers will most likely meet people on the Internet; for example, in a chat room, on MySpace™, on Facebook® or something totally different?

Participant S: MySpace™/Facebook® - Info like birth-days is public and can attract predators

Researcher: Third question, what role do you feel that a teen's personality; for example, A-introverted, B-extroverted or something totally different plays in whether they will meet a predator on the Internet?

Participant S: Introverted. Less likely to tell anyone but chances of meeting predator is the same.

Researcher: Fourth question, please share with me your opinion on the role that teen gratification; for example, sex, companionship, self-esteem, or some-thing else plays in whether a teen will meet an Internet predator?

Participant S: If not interacting with peers they are more likely to act on impulses.

Researcher: Fifth question, please share with me your

opinion on what support would most likely help; for example, more parental supervision, better law enforcement, better High School curriculum or other to prevent teen's contact with an Internet Predator?

Participant S: Everyone's job - Parents are on front line and need to have open dialogue.

Researcher: Sixth question, please share with me your demographic data (sex, number of children, ethnicity).

Participant S: Male/2/Caucasian.

Researcher: Last question, would it be okay to contact you if there are follow on questions?

Participant S: No.

Participant T Interview

Present during interview: Participant T and Researcher

Location of interview: Midwestern United States town High School

Date and time of interview: Monday, February 06, 2012, 1:43 PM

Observation and comment:

INTERVIEW T

Researcher: I would like to conduct short 15-minute interview. The interview will consist of six open-ended questions designed to obtain your opinion on teenage (13 to 17 year-olds) sexual contact with someone whom they meet on the Internet. The interview is designed to learn more about the child's possible motives and Internet tools used which led to the sexual contact. Finally, the interview will explore potential solutions which could reduce the amount of teen sexual contact on the Internet. I have permission from the school district and the principal to conduct the interviews. You will be given a $15 Subway Restaurant Gift Certificate as thanks for participating in the interview.

Researcher: First question, please share with me your opinion on what circumstances most likely lead to teenage sexual encounters with someone whom they meet on the Internet?

Participant T: Naivety/Being seduced/Not knowing who they are talking to.

Researcher: Second question, please share with me your opinion on how teenagers will most likely meet people on the Internet; for example, in a chat room, on MySpace™, on Facebook® or something totally different?

Participant T: Chat Rooms - Kids get bored and need someone to talk to/reach out to.

Researcher: Third question, what role do you feel that a teen's personality; for example, A-introverted, B-extroverted, or something totally different plays in whether they will meet a predator on the Internet?

Participant T: A. Socially awkward/not active in school or sports/not a lot of friends.

Researcher: Fourth question, please share with me your opinion on the role that teen gratification; for example, sex, companionship, self-esteem, or something else plays in whether a teen will meet an Internet predator?

Participant T: Everything plays a role - Combination of experimentation and thrill etc.

Researcher: Fifth question, please share with me your

opinion on what support would most likely help; for example, more parental supervision, better law enforcement, better High School curriculum or other to prevent teen's contact with an Internet Predator?

Participant T: Education - make them understand they do not know who they are talking to.

Researcher: Sixth question, please share with me your demographic data (sex, number of children, ethnicity).

Participant T: Male/2/English.

Researcher: Last question, would it be okay to contact you if there are follow on questions?

Participant T: Yes.

Participant U Interview

Present during interview: Participant U and Researcher

Location of interview: Midwestern United States town High School

Date and time of interview: Monday, February 06, 2012, 1:52 PM

Observation and comment:

Interview U

Researcher: I would like to conduct short 15-minute interview. The interview will consist of six open-ended questions designed to obtain your opinion on teenage (13 to 17 year-olds) sexual contact with someone whom they meet on the Internet. The interview is designed to learn more about the child's possible motives and Internet tools used which led to the sexual contact. Finally, the interview will explore potential solutions which could reduce the amount of teen sexual contact on the Internet. I have permission from the school district and the principal to conduct the interviews. You will be given a $15 Subway Restaurant Gift Certificate as thanks for participating in the interview.

Researcher: First question, please share with me your opinion on what circumstances most likely lead to teenage sexual encounters with someone whom they meet on the Internet?

Participant U: No adult supervision/Left alone with computer and no one around.

Researcher: Second question, please share with me your opinion on how teenagers will most likely meet people on the Internet; for example, in a chat room, on MySpace™, on Facebook® or something totally different?

Participant U: Facebook®/MySpace™. They are on it all the time and do not care who they talk to.

Researcher: Third question, what role do you feel that a teen's personality; for example, A-introverted, B-extroverted or something totally different plays in whether they will meet a predator on the Internet?

Participant U: Does not matter - Depends on whether or not they have positive people in life.

Researcher: Fourth question, please share with me your opinion on the role that teen gratification; for example, sex, companionship, self-esteem, or something else plays in whether a teen will meet an Internet predator?

Participant U: Self esteem is a factor if they are not sure of themselves.

Researcher: Fifth question, please share with me your

opinion on what support would most likely help; for example, more parental supervision, better law enforcement, better High School curriculum or other to prevent teen's contact with an Internet Predator?

Participant U: Parental supervision and more knowledge of how it happens.

Researcher: Sixth question, please share with me your demographic data (sex, number of children, ethnicity).

Participant U: Female/1/Caucasian.

Researcher: Last question, would it be okay to contact you if there are follow on questions?

Participant U: Yes.

Participant V Interview

Present during interview: Participant V and Researcher

Location of interview: Midwestern United States town High School

Date and time of interview: Monday, February 06, 2012, 2:05 PM

Observation and comment:

INTERVIEW V

Researcher: I would like to conduct short 15-minute interview. The interview will consist of six open-ended questions designed to obtain your opinion on teenage (13 to 17 year-olds) sexual contact with someone whom they meet on the Internet. The interview is designed to learn more about the child's possible motives and Internet tools used which led to the sexual contact. Finally, the interview will explore potential solutions which could reduce the amount of teen sexual contact on the Internet. I have permission from the school district and the principal to conduct the interviews. You will be given a $15 Subway Restaurant Gift Certificate as thanks for participating in the interview.

Researcher: First question, please share with me your opinion on what circumstances most likely lead to teenage sexual encounters with someone whom they meet on the Internet?

Participant V: Having time at computer and looking for interaction and something innocent.

Researcher: Second question, please share with me your opinion on how teenagers will most likely meet people on the Internet; for example in a chat room, on MySpace™, on Facebook®, or something totally different?

Participant V: MySpace™/Facebook®/social networking site - They are connected all the time.

Researcher: Third question, what role do you feel that a teen's personality; for example, A-introverted, B-extroverted or something totally different plays in whether they will meet a predator on the Internet?

Participant V: Not restricted to one - introverts could be preyed upon but extroverts could be for thrill.

Researcher: Fourth question, please share with me your opinion on the role that teen gratification; for example, sex, companionship, self-esteem, or something else plays in whether a teen will meet an Internet predator?

Participant V: Self-esteem plays biggest role - predators feed that and keep them involved.

Researcher: Fifth question, please share with me your

opinion on what support would most likely help; for example, more parental supervision, better law enforcement, better High School curriculum or other to prevent teen's contact with an Internet Predator?

Participant V: Parental involvement - Knowing what kids are doing and who they are with.

Researcher: Sixth question, please share with me your demographic data (sex, number of children, ethnicity).

Participant V: Female/0/Caucasian.

Researcher: Last question, would it be okay to contact you if there are follow on questions?

Participant V: Yes.

Participant W Interview

Present during interview: Participant W and Researcher

Location of interview: Midwestern United States town High School

Date and time of interview: Tuesday, February 07, 2012, 4:34 PM

Observation and comment:

INTERVIEW W

Researcher: I would like to conduct short 15-minute interview. The interview will consist of six open-ended questions designed to obtain your opinion on teenage (13 to 17 year-olds) sexual contact with someone whom they meet on the Internet. The interview is designed to learn more about the child's possible motives and Internet tools used which led to the sexual contact. Finally, the interview will explore potential solutions which could reduce the amount of teen sexual contact on the Internet. I have permission from the school district and the principal to conduct the interviews. You will be given a $15 Subway Restaurant Gift Certificate as thanks for participating in the interview.

Researcher: First question, please share with me your opinion on what circumstances most likely lead to teenage sexual encounters with someone whom they meet on the Internet?

Participant W: May have received an email that invites them to visit websites.

Researcher: Second question, please share with me your opinion on how teenagers will most likely meet people on the Internet; for example, in a chat room, on MySpace™, on Facebook® or something totally different?

Participant W: All - School prohibits these sites but that makes them more curious.

Researcher: Third question, what role do you feel that a teen's personality; for example, A-introverted, B-extroverted or something totally different plays in whether they will meet a predator on the Internet?

Participant W: Varies - B needs outside attention but B needs social contact/acceptance.

Researcher: Fourth question, please share with me your opinion on the role that teen gratification; for example, sex, companionship, self-esteem, or something else plays in whether a teen will meet an Internet predator?

Participant W: Kids need acceptance - Sometimes parents and teachers are too busy.

Researcher: Fifth question, please share with me your

opinion on what support would most likely help; for example, more parental supervision, better law enforcement, better High School curriculum or other to prevent teen's contact with an Internet Predator?

Participant W: Parental supervision - Parents are busy working/lots of kids are home alone

Researcher: Sixth question, please share with me your demographic data (sex, number of children, ethnicity).

Participant W: Female/2/Caucasian.

Researcher: Last question, would it be okay to contact you if there are follow on questions?

Participant W: Yes.

Participant X Interview

Present during interview: Participant X and Researcher

Location of interview: Midwestern United States town High School

Date and time of interview: Tuesday, February 07, 2012, 4:41 PM

Observation and comment:

INTERVIEW X

Researcher: I would like to conduct short 15-minute interview. The interview will consist of six open-ended questions designed to obtain your opinion on teenage (13 to 17 year-olds) sexual contact with someone whom they meet on the Internet. The interview is designed to learn more about the child's possible motives and Internet tools used which led to the sexual contact. Finally, the interview will explore potential solutions which could reduce the amount of teen sexual contact on the Internet. I have permission from the school district and the principal to conduct the interviews. You will be given a $15 Subway Restaurant Gift Certificate as thanks for participating in the interview.

Researcher: First question, please share with me your opinion on what circumstances most likely lead to teenage sexual encounters with someone whom they meet on the Internet?

Participant X: Loneliness and boredom.

Researcher: Second question, please share with me your opinion on how teenagers will most likely meet people on the Internet; for example, in a chat room, on MySpace™, on Facebook® or something totally different?

Participant X: Facebook® or Twitter© - they are always talking about them.

Researcher: Third question, what role do you feel that a teen's personality; for example, A-introverted, B-extroverted or something totally different plays in whether they will meet a predator on the Internet?

Participant X: A - Loneliness and they are seeking comfort.

Researcher: Fourth question, please share with me your opinion on the role that teen gratification; for example, sex, companionship, self-esteem, or something else plays in whether a teen will meet an Internet predator?

Participant X: If they are more open to those things they will meet a predator.

Researcher: Fifth question, please share with me your opinion on what support would most likely help; for

example, more parental supervision, better law enforcement, better High School curriculum or other to prevent teen's contact with an Internet Predator?

Participant X: Less access to computer and more access to sports and open gyms.

Researcher: Sixth question, please share with me your demographic data (sex, number of children, ethnicity).

Participant X: Female/0/Caucasian.

Researcher: Last question, would it be okay to contact you if there are follow on questions?

Participant X: Yes, only after 2:30 PM.

Participant Y Interview

Present during interview: Participant Y and Researcher

Location of interview: Transitional housing office area

Date and time of interview: Tuesday, February 07, 2012, 4:56 PM

Observation and comment:

INTERVIEW Y

Researcher: I would like to conduct short 15-minute interview. The interview will consist of six open-ended questions designed to obtain your opinion on teenage (13 to 17 year-olds) sexual contact with someone whom they meet on the Internet. The interview is designed to learn more about the child's possible motives and Internet tools used which led to the sexual contact. Finally, the interview will explore potential solutions which could reduce the amount of teen sexual contact on the Internet. I have permission from the school district and the principal to conduct the interviews. You will be given a $15 Subway Restaurant Gift Certificate as thanks for participating in the interview.

Researcher: First question, please share with me your opinion on what circumstances most likely lead to teenage sexual encounters with someone whom they meet on the Internet?

Participant Y: Kids are so exposed to technology at such an early age and no supervision.

Researcher: Second question, please share with me your opinion on how teenagers will most likely meet people on the Internet; for example, in a chat room, on MySpace™, on Facebook® or something totally different?

Participant Y: All of the above - anywhere kids can post personal information.

Researcher: Third question, what role do you feel that a teen's personality; for example, A-introverted, B-extroverted or something totally different plays in whether they will meet a predator on the Internet?

Participant Y: Both - B is more outgoing but A can be a different person behind computer.

Researcher: Fourth question, please share with me your opinion on the role that teen gratification; for example, sex, companionship, self-esteem, or something else plays in whether a teen will meet an Internet predator?

Participant Y: Peer pressure - Kids are not capable of thinking as adults.

Researcher: Fifth question, please share with me your

opinion on what support would most likely help; for example, more parental supervision, better law enforcement, better High School curriculum or other to prevent teen's contact with an Internet Predator?

Participant Y: Parental Supervision - Parents get busy but teachers can only do so much.

Researcher: Sixth question, please share with me your demographic data (sex, number of children, ethnicity).

Participant Y: Male/0/Caucasian.

Researcher: Last question, would it be okay to contact you if there are follow on questions?

Participant Y: Yes.

Blank page

Transcripts of Pilot Interviews

Pilot 1 Interview

Present during interview: Participant 1 and Researcher

Location of interview: Midwestern United States town High School

Date and time of interview: Thursday, February 02, 2012, 11:28 AM

Observation and comment:

PILOT INTERVIEW 1

Researcher: I would like to conduct short 15-minute interview. The interview will consist of six open-ended questions designed to obtain your opinion on teenage (13 to 17 year-olds) sexual contact with someone whom they meet on the Internet. The interviews are designed to learn more about the child's possible motives and Internet tools used which led to the sexual contact. Finally the interviews will explore potential solutions which could reduce the amount of teen sexual contact on the Internet. I have permission from the school district and the principal to conduct the interviews. You will be given a $15 Subway Restaurant Gift Certificate as thanks for participating in the interviews.

Researcher: First question, please share with me your opinion on what circumstances most likely lead to teenage sexual encounters with someone whom they meet on the Internet?

Pilot 1: Lack of monitoring from parents as to what child is doing.

Researcher: Second question, please share with me your opinion on how teenagers will most likely meet people on the Internet; for example, in a chat room, on MySpace™, on Facebook® or something totally different?

Pilot 1: All of the above mentioned as well as dating websites like eHarmony.

Researcher: Third question, what role do you feel that a teen's personality; for example, A-introverted, B-extroverted or something totally different plays in whether they will meet a predator on the Internet?

Pilot 1: A - More vulnerable and may be only way they feel adequate.

Researcher: Fourth question, please share with me your opinion on the role that teen gratification; for example, sex, companionship, self-esteem, or something else plays in whether a teen will meet an Internet predator?

Pilot 1: Idea of instant gratification - Having everything now.

Researcher: Fifth question, please share with me your opinion on what support would most likely help; for example, more parental supervision, better law enforcement, better High School curriculum or other to prevent teen's contact with an Internet Predator?

Pilot 1: All of the above mentioned as well as talking with peers.

Researcher: Sixth question, please share with me your demographic data (sex, number of children, ethnicity).

Pilot 1: Female/2/Hispanic.

Researcher: Last question, would it be okay to contact you if there are follow on questions?

Pilot 1: Yes.

Pilot 2 Interview
Present during interview: Participant B and Researcher

Location of interview: Midwestern United States town High School

Date and time of interview: Thursday, February 02, 2012, 11:50 AM

Observation and comment:

Pilot 2 Interview
Researcher: I would like to conduct short 15-minute interview. The interview will consist of six open-ended questions designed to obtain your opinion on teenage (13 to 17 year-olds) sexual contact with someone whom they meet on the Internet. The interviews are designed to learn more about the child's possible motives and Internet tools used which led to the sexual contact. Finally the interviews will explore potential solutions which could reduce the amount of teen sexual contact on the Internet. I have permission from the school district and the principal to conduct the interviews. You will be given a $15 Subway Restaurant Gift Certificate as thanks for participating in the interviews.

Researcher: First question, please share with me your opinion on what circumstances most likely lead to teenage sexual encounters with someone whom they meet on the Internet?

Pilot 2: Unregulated internet usage at home and being uneducated about the dangers.

Researcher: Second question, please share with me your opinion on how teenagers will most likely meet people on the Internet; for example, in a chat room, on MySpace™, on Facebook® or something totally different?

Pilot 2: Mainly Facebook® and MySpace™ as they have sort of replaced chat rooms.

Researcher: Third question, what role do you feel that a teen's personality; for example, A-introverted, B-extroverted or something totally different plays in whether they will meet a predator on the Internet?

Pilot 2: A - Teen who is looking to rebel and believes they are mature enough.

Researcher: Fourth question, please share with me your opinion on the role that teen gratification; for example, sex, companionship, self-esteem, or something else plays in whether a teen will meet an Internet predator?

Pilot 2: The fact that it is dangerous but the teen is not aware of the dangers.

Researcher: Fifth question, please share with me your

opinion on what support would most likely help; for example, more parental supervision, better law enforcement, better High School curriculum or other to prevent teen's contact with an Internet Predator?

Pilot 2: Education - health curriculum - but may continue regardless of education.

Researcher: Sixth question, please share with me your demographic data (sex, number of children, ethnicity).

Pilot 2: Male/0/Caucasian.

Researcher: Last question, would it be okay to contact you if there are follow on questions?

Pilot 2: Yes.

Pilot 3 Interview

Present during interview: Participant C and Researcher

Location of interview: Midwestern United States town High School

Date and time of interview: Thursday, February 02, 2012, 12:01 PM

Observation and comment:

PILOT 3 INTERVIEW

Researcher: I would like to conduct short 15-minute interview. The interview will consist of six open-ended questions designed to obtain your opinion on teenage (13 to 17 year-olds) sexual contact with someone whom they meet on the Internet. The interview is designed to learn more about the child's possible motives and Internet tools used which led to the sexual contact. Finally, the interview will explore potential solutions which could reduce the amount of teen sexual contact on the Internet. I have permission from the school district and the principal to conduct the interviews. You will be given a $15 Subway Restaurant Gift Certificate as thanks for participating in the interviews.

Researcher: First question, please share with me your opinion on what circumstances most likely lead to teenage sexual encounters with someone whom they meet on the Internet?

Pilot 3: Facebook® and surfing on the Internet.

Researcher: Second question, please share with me your opinion on how teenagers will most likely meet people on the Internet; for example, in a chat room, on MySpace™, on Facebook® or something totally different?

Pilot 3: Facebook® - They get connected from one friend to another that they do not know.

Researcher: Third question, what role do you feel that a teen's personality; for example, A-introverted, B-extroverted or something totally different plays in whether they will meet a predator on the Internet?

Pilot 3: A - More lonely and looking for friends in another venue.

Researcher: Fourth question, please share with me your opinion on the role that teen gratification; for example, sex, companionship, self-esteem, or something else plays in whether a teen will meet an Internet predator?

Pilot 3: Companionship and friendship in general would play a role.

Researcher: Fifth question, please share with me your opinion on what support would most likely help; for

example, more parental supervision, better law en-forcement, better High School curriculum or other to prevent teen's contact with an Internet Predator?

Pilot 3: More parental supervision and more parent involvement would help.

Researcher: Sixth question, please share with me your demographic data (sex, number of children, ethnicity).

Pilot 3: Female/2/Caucasian.

Researcher: Last question, would it be okay to contact you if there are follow on questions?

Pilot 3: Yes.

Pilot 4 Interview

Present during interview: Participant D and Researcher

Location of interview: Midwestern United States town High School

Date and time of interview: Thursday, February 02, 2012, 12:21 PM

Observation and comment:

PILOT 4 INTERVIEW

Researcher: I would like to conduct short 15-minute interview. The interview will consist of six open-ended questions designed to obtain your opinion on teenage (13 to 17 year-olds) sexual contact with someone whom they meet on the Internet. The interview is designed to learn more about the child's possible motives and Internet tools used which led to the sexual contact. Finally the interviews will explore potential solutions which could reduce the amount of teen sexual contact on the Internet. I have permission from the school district and the principal to conduct the interview. You will be given a $15 Subway Restaurant Gift Certificate as thanks for participating in the interviews.

Researcher: First question, please share with me your opinion on what circumstances most likely lead to teenage sexual encounters with someone whom they meet on the Internet?

Pilot 4: Lack of social skills.

Researcher: Second question, please share with me your opinion on how teenagers will most likely meet people on the Internet; for example, in a chat room, on MySpace™, on Facebook® or something totally different?

Pilot 4: Facebook® - It is more readily available and photos do not have to be authentic.

Researcher: Third question, what role do you feel that a teen's personality; for example, A-introverted, B-extroverted or something totally different plays in whether they will meet a predator on the Internet?

Pilot 4: A - They feel safer with non-verbal contact and they get hooked in.

Researcher: Fourth question, please share with me your opinion on the role that teen gratification; for example, sex, companionship, self-esteem, or something else plays in whether a teen will meet an Internet predator?

Pilot 4: Any kind of attention whether it is negative or positive.

Researcher: Fifth question, please share with me your opinion on what support would most likely help; for

example, more parental supervision, better law enforcement, better High School curriculum or other to prevent teen's contact with an Internet Predator?

Pilot 4: Better parental supervision - Parents have immediate access on home front.

Researcher: Sixth question, please share with me your demographic data (sex, number of children, ethnicity).

Pilot 4: Female/0/Caucasian.

Researcher: Last question, would it be okay to contact you if there are follow on questions?

Pilot 4: Yes.

Pilot 5 Interview

Present during interview: Participant E and Researcher

Location of interview: Midwestern United States town High School

Date and time of interview: Thursday, February 02, 2012, 1:37 PM

Observation and comment:

PILOT 5 INTERVIEW

Researcher: I would like to conduct short 15-minute interview. The interview will consist of six open-ended questions designed to obtain your opinion on teenage (13 to 17 year-olds) sexual contact with someone whom they meet on the Internet. The interview is designed to learn more about the child's possible motives and Internet tools used which led to the sexual contact. Finally, the interview will explore potential solutions which could reduce the amount of teen sexual contact on the Internet. I have permission from the school district and the principal to conduct the interviews. You will be given a $15 Subway Restaurant Gift Certificate as thanks for participating in the interview.

Researcher: First question, please share with me your opinion on what circumstances most likely lead to teenage sexual encounters with someone whom they meet on the Internet?

Pilot 5: Sexualization of society - sex is in our humor and seen as cool positive.

Researcher: Second question, please share with me your opinion on how teenagers will most likely meet people on the Internet; for example, in a chat room, on MySpace™, on Facebook® or something totally different?

Pilot 5: Social networking site or chat room related to something they are into.

Researcher: Third question, what role do you feel that a teen's personality; for example, A-introverted, B-extroverted or something totally different plays in whether they will meet a predator on the Internet?

Pilot 5: Both A and B - Extrovert is more outgoing but introvert has fewer friends.

Researcher: Fourth question, please share with me your opinion on the role that teen gratification; for example, sex, companionship, self-esteem, or something else plays in whether a teen will meet an Internet predator?

Pilot 5: Promiscuity and boredom can lead to it - Also rebelling against parents.

Researcher: Fifth question, please share with me your

opinion on what support would most likely help; for example, more parental supervision, better law enforcement, better High School curriculum or other to prevent teen's contact with an Internet Predator?

Pilot 5: Make sure child is happy and well adjusted and has hobbies.

Researcher: Sixth question, please share with me your demographic data (sex, number of children, ethnicity).

Pilot 5: Male/3/Caucasian.

Researcher: Last question, would it be okay to contact you if there are follow on questions?

Pilot 5: Yes.

Participant Demographics

Participant	Sex	No. of Children	Ethnicity
A	Female	5	Caucasian
B	Male	2	Caucasian
C	Male	0	Caucasian
D	Female	2	Mixed
E	Female	1	Caucasian
F	Female	2	Pacific Islander
G	Female	3	Caucasian
H	Female	1	Caucasian
I	Female	4	Caucasian
J	Female	0	Caucasian
K	Female	1	Caucasian
L	Female	0	African-American
M	Female	0	Hispanic
N	Female	0	Caucasian
O	Female	0	Caucasian
P	Male	0	Caucasian

Participant	Sex	No. of Children	Ethnicity
Q	Male	0	Caucasian
R	Male	2	Caucasian
S	Male	2	Caucasian
T	Male	2	Caucasian
U	Female	1	Caucasian
V	Female	0	Caucasian
W	Female	2	Caucasian
X	Female	0	Caucasian
Y	Male	0	Caucasian

Table 3. Participant Demographics